Nine I

MW00891047

For a
Happy and Successful
Life

Mitchell Earl Gibson, MD
110 Oak Street
High Point NC 27260

Copyright 2011
Tybro Publications

Introduction

During my career as a psychiatrist, I have been given a very privileged view into the lives of thousands of people. One day, I actually took the time to estimate just how many contacts I had witnessed over my tenure as a psychiatrist. I began my residency in 1985, and continued the general practice of clinical psychiatry until June 2005. During that time, I treated people from all walks of life. I worked with governors, astronauts, professional athletes, ambassadors, serial killers, boxers, corporate CEOs, career criminals, children, adolescents, housewives, physicians, millionaires, and countless other people within the human tapestry. I spent years counseling tens of thousands of individuals in nursing homes, hospitals, emergency rooms, homeless shelters, my private office, jails, schools, churches, community centers, adolescent care facilities, and hospice centers. I estimate that I have participated in over 96,000 individual contact sessions with my clients over the past 20 years. This amounts to an average of 20 sessions per day, 5 days per week, and 48 weeks per year over 20 years. This rough estimate does not include on-call nights, weekends, and emergency consultations.

There are many physicians in my field and other walks of medicine who have spent far more time with clients than I have. I personally know that a number of my colleagues treat many times that number of individuals per day. My point here is not to point out how hard medical professionals work. That is part of the arrangement that we accept when we take the oaths and training of a medical professional. I have noted, however, that the tremendous amount of time that we spend delving into the intimate lives of people gives us the opportunity to develop thought-provoking insights into humanity. I will outline these points for you before we proceed.

One: My clients were teaching me more about life than my medical training ever did.

Two: As I watched the sea of humanity parade before me on a daily basis, I often noted how our lives played out like gigantic scenes upon the stage of the world.

Three: Sometimes, when I listened very carefully, a player upon the stage would speak directly to me, and share profound life-changing insight derived from the heart of suffering and desire.

These profound and insightful statements were often repeated at the most unexpected times by the most unlikely clients. I recall one session where one such insight came from a five year old. I was asked to evaluate a young girl who was suspected of being psychotic. Her family reported that she talked to herself, was isolative, and did not sleep well at night because she was afraid of the ghosts that came into her room. After the family had exhausted a number of avenues, including church counselors, psychologists, and family counselors, they brought her in to me for medical evaluation.

The child, Melissa (not her real name), was a beautiful young lady with long, curly golden locks, ruddy cheeks, and large, penetrating blue eyes. She stormed into my office under obvious protest, and sat sullenly in the corner chair as her parents presented her medical history. I noticed that the child would occasionally throw furtive glances at me and just as quickly look away. After her parents had finished giving me her history, I asked them if I could spend a few minutes talking with her alone.

I offered Melissa some of the dolls and stuffed animals from a box that I kept in the corner. She took an almost immediate liking to an old, tattered stuffed bear that lay beside the box. As she stroked the bear's head, she looked up at me and smiled. Then she uttered a statement that floored me.

"Your grandmother says she enjoyed talking with you last night."

I had dreamt about my grandmother the night before. In the dream, my grandmother had cooked a wonderful meal for me, and we'd talked about my work and the family. I remembered the dream because my grandmother had died ten years earlier, before I had graduated from medical school.

"Melissa, how do you know that my grandmother talked with me last night?"

"She told me," Melissa replied plainly.

"How do you know that it was my grandmother, Melissa?"

"Dr. Gibson, we can do this like all my other counselors, or you can empty your cup a little and really listen to me."

Her words hit me like a blinding flash of light in a dark cave. This child was experiencing perceptions that she could not share with others. If I continued along a cold, clinical psychiatric line of questioning, I would most likely hospitalize her, place her on anti-psychotic medication, and turn off the unique light that burned within her consciousness forever. If I listened to her, emptying my cup so to speak, I learned that I would have to accept my role in the creation of something wonderful.

We talked for 30 minutes. She explained her visions and communications with the "people in the dream," as she called them. As we talked, I realized that she was not psychotic. Melissa was a budding clairvoyant. I never gave her medication, and through our work together, she learned to control her gift and grew into a happy, healthy young lady.

Her insight into her own dilemma was profound. There have been many "aha" moments in my clinical career that mirror the empty-your-cup perspective provided to me by Melissa. This book was inspired by the gift of thousands of such moments.

The Nine Insights is a book that is designed to be a guide for those who wish to rise above the suffering and confusion that so often marks this path of existence. As a medical professional, the Creator has given me thousands of profound moments of transformational insight. I began keeping notes on these insights, and stored them away in a journal that, over time, became the basis for this work. From time to time, I shared these insights with friends, family, clients, and colleagues. Simple in their presentation, profound in their scope, *The Nine Insights* are meant only as a reference. Each chapter presents one insight as a unique entity. The stories and vignettes that support each insight are, in large part, based on my personal clinical experiences. From time to time, I have included a number of famous stories from history that help to outline the deeper perspectives of some of the insights.

I invite the reader to share these insights with others. I hope to provide a little light in a world in which millions feel isolated, empty, and without hope. *The Nine Insights* came from the Creator. I believe that they are His way of reminding each of us that we are unique and special to Him in ways that we cannot even imagine.

Mitchell Earl Gibson, MD

THE JOKE'S ON YOU by Phil Ryder & **YOU**

"So I see you finally got off the couch and decided to join me."

- Chopper • Melrose, MA

Insight Number One

Regularly giving away a small portion of your wealth helps to prevent the energy of chaos from building up in your life.

Money is one of the single greatest motivating forces for much of what we do in life. It is true that some of us are not motivated by the acquisition of money or wealth. Some people have more than they will ever need. Some people have no need for wealth. However, that is not true of most people. Most people are taught that getting the right education, securing the right job, and managing your finances properly are the secrets to a prosperous life. That is the real reason that most of us work. That is the real reason that most of us went to college. That is the real reason that most people get up every day and repeat the same routines that our forefathers did before us. In short, we want the security that money brings to life. We want security for our children.

Few of us, however, really stop to consider the effect that bringing all that money into our life will have on the energy of our life.

Money is energy. Think about it for a second. Where is the money that you made last week right now? If you have already received your paycheck, you might quickly say that it's sitting in a bank account. If so, then the money is sitting in a virtual digital state. That is, you can't put in into your hands unless you physically go to a bank, withdraw it, and place it in your wallet or purse. Otherwise, the money exists in an electronic state with which you will likely never interact physically. The electronic state is fine for paying bills, writing checks, paying the mortgage, using your debit card etc. Most of us don't use much cash these days. However, the money that you use is there when you need it physically. Otherwise, it is only energy.

You might then say, "Well, if I took all of my money out of the bank and used only cash, then it is physical." Consider this, the physical money that you have in your hand is a note, essentially a guarantee to pay debt. It is backed by the energy of the government that issued the note. Without that government's backing, more energy, the note is worthless. Granted, most governments place considerable energy into backing their notes; but, again, the physical money that you now have in your hand is backed by energy. Without that energy, the note is just paper.

Now, let us take the analysis one step further. Let us use money as one important measure of wealth in general. There are others of course: land, precious metals, commodities, etc.; but for the sake of our discussion, let us stick to cash for the moment. Mankind has been creating wealth for a very long time. Scientists have dated the use of coined money in human society back to 700 B.C. The Electrum stater turtle coin, coined at Aegina island, is one of the first examples of metallic money ever found. Electrum coins were also introduced about 650 B.C. in Lydia.

Have you ever stopped to consider how most of mankind's wealth has been generated in the world for the last 2000 years? Mankind is a creature of habit. The means by which he has generated wealth tends to be related to a number of habits that we don't like to think about, but which are, nevertheless, among our prime indulgences. Forget the Fortune 500, forget sports, forget Wall Street. The ways that are most profitable are probably not at the top of your list. Let's examine them.

5. The Drug Trade

The trade of drugs has existed for as long as drugs have existed. However, the trade of drugs was fully legal until the introduction of drug prohibition. The history of the illegal drug trade is thus closely tied to the history of drug prohibition. In the First Opium War, the United Kingdom forced China to allow British merchants to trade opium with the general population of China. Although illegal by imperial decree, smoking opium had become common in the 1800s due to increasing importation via British merchants. Trading in opium was (as the heroin trade is today) extremely lucrative. As a result of the trade, an estimated two million Chinese people became addicted to the drug.

The British Crown (via the treaties of Nanking and Tianjin) took vast sums of money from the Chinese government in what they referred to as 'reparations' for the wars. The illegal drug trade is operated similarly to other underground markets. Various drug cartels specialize in separate processes along the supply chain, often localized to maximize production efficiency, and minimize damage caused by law enforcement. Depending on the profitability of each layer, cartels usually vary in size, consistency, and organization.

The chain ranges from low-level street dealers—who may be individual drug users themselves—through street gangs and contractor-like middle men, up to multinational empires that rival governments in size. A UN report stated that the global drug trade generated an estimated $321.6 billion in 2003.

Of course, the estimates largely depend upon the amount of the drug trade that may be reported by authorities. The actual monetary amounts are likely to be far higher. Hundreds of billions of dollars every year are filtered through the drug trade. With this illicit trade comes the energy of an untold number of crimes perpetuated by those who sell the drugs and those who buy the drugs. Each one of those acts creates a pocket of energy that attaches itself to every dollar created in the drug trade.

4. Human Slavery

Human slavery is a form of forced labor in which people are considered to be the property of others. Slaves can be held against their will from the time of their capture, purchase, or birth, and deprived of the right to leave, to refuse to work, or to demand wages. In some societies, it was legal for an owner to kill a slave; in others, it was a crime.

The organization Anti-Slavery International defines slavery as "forced labour." By this definition, there are approximately 27 million slaves in the world today; more than at any point in history, and more than twice as many as all African slaves brought to the Americas combined.

The International Labour Organization (ILO), however, does not equate forced labor with slavery. According to the ILO, there are an estimated 12 million people around the world still working under coercion in forced labor, slavery, and slavery-like practices.

Most are debt slaves, largely in South Asia, who are under debt bondage incurred by lenders, some for generations. Human trafficking is mostly for prostituting women and children into the sex trade. It is described as "the largest slave trade in history," and is the fastest growing criminal industry, set to outgrow drug trafficking. Slavery is one of the oldest professions in the world.

Many of the great civilizations on this planet, including America, depended upon the labor of slaves for centuries. Each and every time that a slave was bought, sold, or forced into unpaid labor, those acts created packets of energy that affected wealth. Since these acts have been ongoing for thousands of years, one can safely say that the energy of slavery has touched a large part of the wealth of this world.

3. The Sex Trade

Sex is one of the oldest and most profitable businesses in the history of the planet. Every day, hundreds of thousands of transactions related to sex and sexual activity take place in the world. Most of this activity is illegal and is never reported. It has been suggested that human sex trafficking is the fastest growing form of contemporary slavery, and is the third largest and fastest growing criminal industry in the world.

"Annually, according to U.S. Government-sponsored research completed in 2006, approximately 800,000 people are trafficked across national borders, which does not include millions trafficked within their own countries. Approximately 80 percent of transnational victims are women and girls and up to 50 percent are minors," reports the US Department of State in a 2008 study. Due to the illegal and underground nature of sex trafficking, the exact extent of women and children forced into prostitution is unknown.

Children are sold into the global sex trade every year. They are often kidnapped or orphaned, and are sometimes sold by their own families. According to the International Labour Organization, the problem is especially alarming in Thailand, the Philippines, Sri Lanka, Vietnam, Cambodia, Nepal, and India.

Poverty, social exclusion, and war are at the heart of human trafficking. Some women are hoodwinked into believing promises of a better life, sometimes by people who are known to, and trusted by, them. Traffickers may own legitimate travel agencies, modeling agencies, and employment offices in order to gain women's trust. Others are simply kidnapped. Once overseas, it is common for their passport to be confiscated by the trafficker, and for them to be warned of the consequences should they attempt to escape. Such consequences include beatings, rape, threats of violence against their families, and death threats. It is common, particularly in Eastern Europe, that should they manage to return to their families, they will only be trafficked once again.

Globally, forced labor generates $31 billion dollars annually, half of it in the industrialized world, and a tenth in transition countries, according to the International Labour Organization in a report on forced labour ("A Global Alliance Against Forced Labour", ILO, 11 May 2005). Trafficking in people has been facilitated by porous borders and advanced communication technologies. It has become increasingly transnational in scope and highly lucrative within its barbarity.

According to a report by the UN Office on Drugs and Crime, the most common destinations for victims of human trafficking are Thailand, Japan, Israel, Belgium, the Netherlands, Germany, Italy, Turkey, and the United States. Due to the illicit nature of the business, it is difficult to estimate the true impact of the sex trade on the world's wealth. Once again, however, each illegal act related to the sex trade creates energy that has an effect on the world's wealth.

2. Gambling

Gambling is one of the oldest known pursuits of mankind. Archeological evidence suggests that even the earliest caveman was a gambler. Dice-like objects made from the ankle bone of a sheep or dog, called Astragali, dating back 40,000 years, have been found. Cave drawings depicting gambling offer further proof of the existence of early gamblers. Pairs of dice have even turned up in the ruins of Pompeii; some of them "loaded" to fall a certain way.

Around 2,300 B.C., the Chinese invented a game of chance using tiles, and 1,100 years later, Greek soldiers amused themselves with dice games, though, in ancient Greece, gambling was illegal. In Egypt, a pair of ivory dice was found in Thebes dating back to 1,500 B.C., and ancient gambling artifacts have been unearthed in China, Japan, India, and Rome.

In ancient Rome, Claudius redesigned his carriage so that he would have more room to throw dice. Caligula confiscated knights' property to cover his gambling debts, and Roman soldiers gambled for the robes of Christ after his crucifixion. At the height of the Roman Empire, lawmakers decreed that all children were to be taught to gamble and throw dice.

During the 14th century, and in spite of being an inveterate gambler himself, King Henry VIII outlawed gambling when he discovered that his soldiers spent more time gambling than improving their battle skills. When Henry's wife, Anne Boleyn, and her brother were tried for treason and incest, the odds were 10-to-1 on acquittal.

In the New World, Native Americans, believing that the gods themselves invented games of chance, played dice with plum stones painted white or black. In addition to wagering possessions, Native Americans also played to predict future harvests, and in hopes of curing seriously ill tribal members.

During the Revolutionary War, lotteries bankrolled the Continental Army. Washington himself bought the first ticket for a federal lottery in 1793, sponsored to finance improvements in the District of Columbia, and nearly all state governments sanctioned lotteries. By the 1830s, more than 420 lotteries nationwide offered prizes. Lotteries remained a popular fundraising method throughout the 18th and 19th centuries.

Riverboats and frontier towns in the New World emerged, providing new gambling venues, sometimes legal, sometimes not. And one risked much more than a few gold pieces when gambling in the frontier days. Card cheats and conmen were often lynched, denoting the public's attitude toward professional gamblers, or "sharpers" as they were often known.

In the 1830s, refugee sharpers from the South moved to Cincinnati and opened the nation's first "Wolf-Traps" or "10 Percent Houses", named for the house's cut of the action. Cincinnati was also the birthplace of the "Horse-Hair game", a method for cheating in cards by which a player, aided by an accomplice's distractions, manipulated cards and chips by the use of a horse hair attached to a vest button.

After the Civil War, evangelical reform wiped out most of the lotteries. In the 1890s, the flagrant fraud of the nationally marketed Louisiana lottery led Congress to outlaw the remaining games, creating public disdain for lotteries, and in 1910, Nevada made it a felony to operate a gambling game.

Prohibition sent drinking and gambling underground. But it didn't stay down for long. In the 1930s, restrictions eased up and legalized betting on horse racing became popular. In 1931, Nevada legalized gambling again, and casinos literally sprouted from the sands of the desert. Atlantic City followed suit in 1978 and, since then, other states have legalized various forms of gambling.

Today, when a casino counts money, it often does so by weighing it. The energy of gambling has affected the wealth of this world for thousands of years. Each and every act of gambling issues more of this energy into the world's money supply.

1. War

War is a constant in human society. War can be seen as a growth of economic competition in a competitive international system. Based on this view, wars begin as a pursuit of markets for natural resources and wealth. While this theory has been applied to many conflicts, such counter arguments become less valid as the increasing mobility of capital and information level the distributions of wealth worldwide, or when considering that it is relative, not absolute, wealth differences that may fuel wars. Once a war has ended, the losing nations are sometimes required to pay war reparations to the victorious nations. In certain cases, land is ceded to the victorious nations. For example, the territory of Alsace-Lorraine has been traded between France and Germany on three different occasions.

Typically speaking, war becomes very intertwined with the economy, and many wars are partially or entirely based on economic reasons, such as the American Civil War. In some cases, war has stimulated a country's economy (World War II is often credited with bringing America out of the Great Depression), but in many cases, such as the wars of Louis XIV, the Franco-Prussian War, and World War I, warfare serves only to damage the economy of the countries involved. For example, Russia's involvement in World War I took such a toll on the Russian economy that it almost collapsed, and this greatly contributed to the start of the Russian Revolution of 1917.

One of the starkest illustrations of the effect of war upon economies is the Second World War. The Great Depression of the 1930s ended as nations increased their production of war materials to serve the war effort. The financial cost of World War II is estimated at about U.S.1,944 billion dollars worldwide, making it the most costly war in capital as well as lives.

In the Soviet Union, property damage inflicted by the Axis invasion was estimated at a value of 679 billion rubles. The combined damage consisted of complete or partial destruction of 1,710 cities and towns, 70,000 villages/hamlets, 2,508 church buildings, 31,850 industrial establishments, 40,000 miles of railroad, 4,100 railroad stations, 40,000 hospitals, 84,000 schools, and 43,000 public libraries.

When one examines the economic cost of war, the physical cost must also be examined. War spreads disease and suffering on an untold scale. Every dollar that is spent on war extracts an enormous amount of chaotic energy that affects the wealth of the world.

War, gambling, sex, slavery, and the drug trade dwarf all other wealth-making enterprises on this planet. Unfortunately, each of these endeavors creates a tremendous amount of suffering, pain, and chaos in its wake. This energy then becomes part of every dollar that is created.

Now, let us examine the effect that this energy might have on each of us on a personal level. If you place a bowl of fruit on the counter, the fruit will sit undisturbed for some time. The fruit will last longer, however, if there are no rotten or diseased pieces in the bowl. If you deliberately introduce a rotten piece into the bowl, the rot will spread throughout the bowl and cause the other pieces to spoil more quickly.

This same principle applies to every dollar that you earn. Examine the list of wealth-making enterprises that we outlined earlier. All of these enterprises have tainted the energy of the wealth of this world in a negative way.

In other words, the energy of every dollar that you receive has the stain of drugs, slavery, sex, gambling, and war.

Each and every time we receive money in this world, we also accept a small part of this energy stain into our lives. The energy of chaos, disease, suffering, and pain that is part of the wealth of this world is spread through our contact with wealth. To be sure, one needs money and wealth in order to live and conduct many affairs in our world. This brings us to the first insight:

Regularly giving away a small portion of your wealth helps to prevent the energy of chaos from building up in your life.

One theory regarding the origin of suffering, chaos, and pain in this world is that it enters into our lives through our decisions and actions. The theory simply states that good and constructive actions and decisions bring beneficial results into your life. Destructive acts and decisions theoretically bring destructive energy into your life. Some people call this karma. In this sense, money becomes one of the mediums through which the energy of karma is spread from one person to another.

By holding on to all of the energy that money brings into our lives, we may inadvertently be holding on to the negative karmic energy that comes with it. Mind you, only a small amount of this energy is necessary in order for it to affect your life. Chaotic karmic energy has power.
Remember the bowl of fruit. Imagine that your life is the bowl. Now, add a bit of the chaotic force from wealth into that bowl.

Think about it for a moment; what would the energy of war, drugs, or gambling look like if it manifested in your life? Would it become an illness? A car accident? Loss of a job?

Family tensions? Chaos in a relationship?
Bankruptcy?

Many religions teach that giving away a
small portion of your wealth through a
process known as tithing is important for
spiritual and emotional reasons. However,
most religions never fully explain why we
should follow this rule. Perhaps one reason
that we should consider this principle relates
to the first insight. Regularly giving away a
small portion of your wealth can help to
prevent the buildup of negative chaotic
energy in your life.

Remember the bowl of fruit. If you notice a
rotting piece of fruit in the bowl and remove
it from the others, the rest last longer. The
same may be said to be true of our lives. If
we regularly give away the energy of chaos,
that has the potential to spoil our lives, we
can then prevent the good energy in life
from being affected by the bad energy.

Some spiritual teachers maintain that by donating 10-15% of your wealth to others, you will clear the energy of your life from the influence of negative forces. They caution that holding on to wealth too tightly causes these forces to build and make us sick. To be fair, there are many people who cannot afford to give that much to others. There are many people who live from one paycheck to the next. What can they do to avoid this energy?

Money is not the only commodity of value that we own. Each of us in our own way possesses something of value that we can share and give to others. For some of us, that might be time. Donating a portion of our time on a regular basis for the benefit of others is one way of giving of your wealth. Working at a shelter, visiting the sick and shut in, or volunteering at a daycare center are all ways that one may share one's wealth without spending money. Donating a possession or a service is another way of sharing your wealth.

Allowing the negative chaotic energy to be removed from your life also has another unexpected benefit. Nature abhors a vacuum. If one removes negative energy from a system, this leaves room for positive energy to reenter the system. Instead of fighting off disease, chaos, and suffering related to negative energy, the system would then have more time and energy to process the power of blessings. In this way, giving to others is a powerful method of creating blessings in your own life.

Insight Number Two

The energy of your life will be consumed by the forces of chaos and order. The choices that you make will determine which force dominates your life.

Evelyn Ashmole was born in Brewster, Nebraska; population 29. Brewster was a small town by any standard, and Evelyn's primary hope throughout her entire childhood was to grow up, leave Brewster, go to college, and live in the big city. She wanted to get a job with a large company, just like the ones that she saw on television. In Brewster, everyone farmed, and those who did not work, did not eat. Evelyn loved her little town, her four brothers, two sisters, and her mother and father. She loved the white-tile Baptist church that they went to each Sunday, and the loving elderly pastor who had taught there for more than 40 years. As she saw it, her childhood was as close to perfect as she could imagine.

Evelyn grew up and performed well enough in high school to earn a scholarship to the University of Nebraska. She earned a degree in library science and, after college, took a job in Phoenix as a clerk at the Arizona State University library. She had continued to attend church every Sunday, talked to her parents faithfully every week, and managed to make some happy and constructive friendships which helped to quell some of the loneliness that she felt when she thought about home. Evelyn's life was not quite perfect, however.

Over the past three years, Evelyn had attracted a string of relationships with men that had nearly killed her. Bill, one of her boyfriends, a junior architect at a local firm, had tried to throw her out of his car when she refused to have sex with him. The car was moving at 50 miles per hour at the time. Prior to that, he had threatened to hit her on several occasions, and was frequently verbally abusive.

David, her first boyfriend, had stalked her after she decided that she no longer wanted to see him. Several times, she found him lurking behind the bushes at her home late at night as she prepared for bed. She reported him to the police, but he always managed to escape before they came to investigate. With no witnesses and no proof, they had nothing to go on. Eventually, he moved to Los Angeles and sent her a scathing letter stating that she had ruined his life, and that he never wanted to see her again.

The incident that drove her to see me, however, was quite a bit more serious than the scenes outlined above. One night, as she walked to her car, Evelyn noticed that someone was following her. She worked the late shift at the library, and she often asked one of the security guards to escort her to the parking deck. On this night, however, she was in a hurry to get home to talk to her oldest sister Ann about her upcoming wedding. Ann was the first of the three girls to get married in the family. In her haste, she had forgotten to call for an escort.

Evelyn looked over her shoulder and saw a tall, thin young man quickly approaching her. She did not recognize him and instinctively clutched her purse tightly and slipped her hand into the outer compartment. Just before the young man could overtake her, she grabbed the container of mace that she had secreted away in her palm, sprayed him in the face, and ran to her car. The young man covered his face and grimaced in pain. Her quick thinking slowed him down just enough so that she could get to her car, lock the door, and speed away without further incident. She began having nightmares, panic attacks, and problems sleeping. A couple of weeks later, she called my office for an appointment.

Evelyn was almost certain that something was wrong with her. She wanted to know why she had such bad luck with men. She was afraid that she was going crazy. We talked for a couple of sessions and, except for recent events, Evelyn Ashmole was as healthy and well-adjusted as any young woman I had ever met. One day at the beginning of our session, Evelyn noticed a textbook of forensic psychiatry on my shelf.

"I didn't know you were into this stuff, Doctor Gibson."

"Oh you mean forensics. Why yes, I trained in forensic psychiatry during my residency, and I consult for the police, banks, and the court system from time to time on forensic cases. Why do you ask?"

"I just love reading about true crime, novels mostly."

"How many books of that type would you say that you have read, Evelyn?"

"Oh hundreds and hundreds. I started reading them when I was in college, just a little bit now and then. But as luck would have it, the section that I work in at ASU is full of them. When things are slow, I get to read as many as I like."

Evelyn went on to describe her hobby in more detail. She not only read true crime novels, she had developed an insatiable appetite for them. Her favorites were based on serial killers, gangsters, sex crimes, and rape. Her favorite movies were of the same genre, and each night before she went to sleep, she rewarded herself with a movie from her vast collection of horror, true crime, and mystery.

"So, Evelyn, what effect do you think these books and movies have on your life?"

"They are just that — books and movies. They don't affect me. I am a good person and I don't think of myself that way. Why do you ask?"

"I find it very curious that the troubling events in your otherwise very placid life are quite similar to the energy that you pour into your mind through your books and movies."

"But how can there be any connection between the two? I mean, it's not like I advertise to the creeps out there what I read and look at on TV. How would they know anything about the choices that I make in my mental diet?"

At that moment, Evelyn's rather insightful comment struck me like a ton of bricks. She was right. Her passion for true crime and horror was her little secret. She didn't share it with her family, close friends, or coworkers. As a matter of fact, Evelyn had decided to keep her indulgence in crime all to herself, but she was not sure why. Her mental and emotional diet was, for the most part, quite healthy, except for the plate of unhealthy relationships that she had served herself.

Evelyn's comment about her mental diet had triggered a chain of thoughts in my consciousness that led to the second insight in this book.

Insight Two

The energy of your life will be consumed by the forces of chaos and order. The choices that you make will determine which force dominates.

Our understanding of reality has changed drastically over the last 40 years. At the start of the twentieth century, Newtonian physics and the atomic model of reality dominated our schools and textbooks. The revolution of relativity, quantum physics, and Albert Einstein changed all that forever. We now know that reality as we perceive it is a creation of the mind, and that everything that we see exists only while we are looking directly at it. That means that the book you are now holding exists only while you are looking at it. Your home, your car, your body, and everything that you see and perceive in the world around you exists only because your consciousness creates the perception of seeing it. Experiments in quantum physics have shown that the fundamental particles that make up our reality are profoundly influenced by how we perceive them. These experiments have shown that even at the subatomic level of reality, particles of matter can be influenced by our perceptions and consciousness.

In our younger days, we were taught that a rock is a rock, a tree is a tree, and a cloud is a cloud, no matter who looks at them. The reality is, no two people perceive reality in exactly the same way. As a matter of fact, each of us shapes reality around us according to our emotions, perceptions, and choices. This brings us to Evelyn.

Evelyn's choices in life were, for the most part, very healthy and constructive. However, she had planted within the sphere of her consciousness, a menu of unhealthy energies, which ultimately led to the growth of a series of negative changes in the world around her. In the books and movies that she loved to read, women tended to be victimized by men in often violent and deadly ways. Evelyn had grown up in a healthy and loving family, and her appetite for true crime novels was far different than the energy that had shaped her youth.

As she explored her independence in life, Evelyn naturally desired to engage in relationships with men and find her true love. However, she had not dated in high school, and she had had only one relationship in college. She was still somewhat naive in matters relating to men and, much to her surprise, a great deal of her "experience" with the energy of relationships had been found in her books. *Without realizing it, Evelyn had programmed her subconscious mind to resonate with violent and unhealthy themes relating to men.* As a result, she had shaped her growing relationship consciousness with energies that tended to resonate with the forces of chaos and crime when she interacted with men.

"So by reading about crime, you think I attract it to myself?"

"It is a theory. I would like to test it, Evelyn."

"How can we test it?"

"I believe that the mind is very powerful; much more powerful than we can imagine. I would like you to stop reading about true crime, murder, and mystery novels. I want you to transfer from the department you currently work in, and try something different. Tell them you are bored or something like that."

"But what will I read? What will I do with myself? How will I get to sleep?"

"By programming your consciousness with negative energy, you are attracting to yourself the kinds of people and events that you may not want. Why not try reading more uplifting and positive books? A good romance perhaps...one with happy healthy heroines and heroes who get the girl and don't kill her."

"This sounds a little crazy. You really think my mind is doing all that?"

"Let's look at it this way. We all get a certain amount of energy in life that we can spend in any way that we choose. If you choose to spend it on chaos and suffering, we will get more chaos at the end of the day. If we choose to spend it on order and happiness, we will create events that lead to happiness and order. The choice is yours."

Evelyn took my advice and cleaned out her collection. She transferred to the children's section at the library, and gradually fell into a happy and uneventful routine. She began to sleep better, and her nightmares vanished entirely. Over the next few months, she noticed that her mood improved, her anxiety problems disappeared, and she felt better about herself. She felt that a cloud was beginning to lift from her thinking.

From time to time, she would slip back and read a crime novel or two, but she noticed that her sleep would inevitably become disturbed, and the nightmares would return. She made the connection that the energy that she placed within her mental diet would indeed manifest in her life.

Evelyn soon met a healthy young man, a professor in sociology at ASU, and she is very happy. There has been no report of violence or chaos in her relationship, and as far as she is concerned, reading true crime, mystery novels, and looking at horror movies is strictly off limits.

Evelyn Ashmole learned the basics of a very important key to leading a happy and fulfilling life. The energy of consciousness that we build into our lives draws upon a discrete well of potential. This force can and will manifest in our lives according to our choices. If we seek out happy, constructive, and harmonious choices, those energies will grow into events in our lives which will lead to happiness, harmony, and contentment. If we seek out chaotic, unhealthy, and negative choices on a regular basis, those energies will grow into events in our lives which will lead to disharmony, unhappiness, and misfortune.

THE JOKE'S ON YOU   by Phil Ryder & **YOU**

© 2011 Phil Ryder · www.thefunnypages.com

Hyena Youngman was the only one to find his one-liners funny.

- edberger · NY, NY

Insight Number Three

Life is an exercise in the creation of a menu of possibilities.

Most of us go through life with one goal in mind. We seek to make acquaintances with people who will make a difference in our lives. We often do this through gathering at social events, churches, schools, mosques, synagogues, bars, movies, sporting events, and numerous other venues that will hopefully allow us to make contact with people who are special to us. By design, humans are social animals. There are literally hundreds of miles of open land in just about every country in the world. If you drive over this land or fly above it, you will find one striking and repetitive theme — humans tend to build their homes close together. No matter how much space we have available to us, we tend to find ways to stay close to each other. No matter the continent, no matter the culture, no matter the era, this is what we do. If you can find an individual who chooses to live completely alone in the world, it is so rare that it confirms the reality that human beings need to live amongst each other. We are compelled from within ourselves to group together. Humans are social animals; it is our nature to be so. But why do we do this? Why are we so compelled to live in groups?

At the most basic level, we are drawn together for reproduction. Built into every human being is the need to reproduce. This need, and the means to do it, is not taught; it just is. Such a built-in need to reproduce others of one's own kind is basic to all living things, be it a flower or a dolphin. We could survive living alone in a hut or a cave, but our species would soon die out if enough of us chose to do that. As a matter of fact, the growth and expansion of our species depends upon our ability to make relationships work.

This growth and expansion is the core reason for the existence of civilization. We build things as a matter of survival, and because it is part of our nature to express ourselves through building. We also build events into our lives as part of the expression of the energy of being. In this regard, we could build events alone. But this brings us back to a core truth about who we are as humans; the growth and expansion of our species depends upon our ability to work together. This concept brings us to the third insight:

Insight Three

Life is an exercise in the creation of a menu of possibilities.

When we closely examine the human tendency to live together, we quickly realize that all that closeness brings with it an infinite range of possible interactions. These interactions bring with them a menu of possibilities for growth, change, and evolution. Linda, a client whom I was treating for depression, once told me about a dream that she had that changed her life.

In the dream, she was a talk show host, and she saw herself interviewing two very famous politicians onstage. As she talked with them, she noticed that one of the guests kept changing into other people. One moment she was herself, but during the course of the show, she would assume the appearance of a number of famous and influential people. At first, my client tried not to pay attention to the changes, but one change caught her eye. The guest, who at one moment was Abraham Lincoln, and the next moment Babe Ruth, eventually changed into a large, life-like statue of Winnie the Pooh. In the dream, Linda stopped the interview, looked directly at the guest, and asked her why she had chosen to change her appearance in this way. The guest (as Winnie the Pooh) sat up, smiled, and explained to Linda the reason for the transition.

"I recognized that you were really enjoying the show tonight, but you weren't really seeing why you created it in the first place."

"What do you mean?" Linda remarked to the bear.

"This dream, this set, is your creation. You set all of this up for a reason."

"Would you care to enlighten me as to why I set this up, Mr. Winnie the Pooh?"

The bear smirked and grinned to itself. In the blink of an eye, it changed itself into a reasonable facsimile of Oprah Winfrey.

"I think you will listen more closely if I take this form. You see, you really hate your job, but you are afraid to take the first step in doing something about it. You created this show as a way of giving yourself the answer to your dilemma."

"I don't get it. Sure, I do hate my boring, low-paying job at the copy desk downtown. What I would really like to do is something like this I suppose..."

"Exactly! That's it. What you really want to do is to fully examine your menu of life possibilities, and see what you have built into it."

"I do that all the time, and it only gets me a list of dreams and wishes, I can't pay my bills with them."

"And that brings me to my point. You need to understand that life is an exercise in the creation of a menu of possibilities. Everyone is given the same possibilities, but not the same choices. There are people around you who can open doors for you, Linda. All you need do is knock."

In that moment, the Oprah dream character got up from her chair, grabbed Linda, and gave her a big hug. She smiled, kissed her on the cheek, and looked her in the eye.

"When you wake up, Linda, I want you to remember what I am about to say. People bring events into your life, if you let them. Open one of the doors that exist all around you and walk through it."

Linda was puzzled by the dream for weeks, and sought my help in an attempt to unravel its mystery. We soon came to the realization that she was indeed unhappy with her job, and that her real goal in life was to become a talk show host. However, at age 48, with no previous experience, she felt unsure of her ability to realize that dream.

Oddly enough, we discovered that she had made a series of demo tapes demonstrating her skill as an interviewer and talk show host. We looked at the tapes together. Linda had sent the tapes in to a number of radio stations, television networks, and cable shows. None of them had bothered to write back.

I noted that she did indeed have skill as an interviewer, but something was missing. In and of itself, Linda interviewing a guest on the tape was not very compelling. Then an idea occurred to me that broke the ice and helped to solve the mystery of the dream.

"Linda, have you ever thought of sharing the stage with another person as your co-host?"

"I guess not. I always saw myself as kind of an Oprah Winfrey solo kinda gal."

"Do you know anyone who might be interested in cutting a demo tape with you, as your co-host?"

"Now that you mention it, my friend Lysandra has been bugging me about doing something together. She likes to write and she helped me put together some of my tapes."

"Would she help you as a co-host if you asked?"

Linda did ask her friend to help her. As luck would have it, Linda's chemistry with Lysandra was fantastic. The new demo tapes that they created sparkled with life, energy, and humor. They sent the tapes in to the same venues, and within weeks they received a call from two cable television shows. The producers loved the chemistry between the two women. They now have a nationally syndicated talk show on cable television. Incidentally, Linda later learned that Lysandra had a large collection of Winnie the Pooh stuffed toys!

Linda learned that despite all of her hard work, the window of possibilities that she wanted to open for herself simply refused to budge. She learned that she needed to join forces with another talented person in order to open that window. Linda discovered a powerful and essential insight to achieving happiness and prosperity in this world. She discovered the principle of destiny pairing.

People do indeed bring events into our lives. Creating happy and prosperous events often requires that we expand our menu of possibilities, and seek out the skills and talents of like-minded individuals. The universe enjoys pairing us with people, or even groups, that bring out the best in us.

Simon and Garfunkel was one of the essential groups of the late 1960s and early 1970s, and one of folk rock's most successful groups of all time. Simon and Garfunkel enjoyed success as both singers and songwriters. Their songs, "Sound of Silence", "Mrs. Robinson", and "Bridge Over Troubled Water" helped them to reach the peak of their success by 1970.

In the middle to late 1960s, the married couple of Sonny and Cher became household names and sex symbols for the hippie generation. Their most famous song "I Got You Babe" won them widespread fame and is still widely recognizable to this day by members of all generations due to its inclusion in a wide variety of movies and television programs. When their musical career began to fade, Sonny and Cher tried to revive their careers by a short-lived and largely unsuccessful attempt at starring in a couple of movies together. They did have a successful run at a television show together, but when their marriage failed publicly in 1974, they parted ways professionally as well. Cher went on to success as a movie star, and Sonny Bono became a Congressman from California until his untimely death in a skiing accident in 1998.

Possibly one of the most recognized comic duos since the 1970s, Richard "Cheech" Marin and Tommy Chong have filled television and movie screens with acts of stupidity and excessive drug and alcohol consumption. Cheech and Chong's first full length movie was *Up In Smoke*. The movie debuted in 1978, and is even recognized by today's newer generations.

Laurel and Hardy is another one of those duos that is still a part of popular culture to this day. The duo joined forces in the 1920s and was seen together into the 1950s. They acted together in both silent and talking short films and feature-length films, including *Lucky Dog*, *Sons of the Desert*, *Way Out West*, and *Block-Heads*.

Abbott and Costello was one of the most famous duos of all time. The words "Who's on First?" best characterize the memory of Abbott and Costello as their most famous routine, still repeated to this day on television and in films. Their careers saw them moving through the burlesque stage, to radio, and finally to television. From 1936 until their amicable split in 1957, the pair was widely known as the kings of comedy.

Famous duos have graced our world in business, art, politics, writing, and many other arenas. Bill Gates and Paul Allen founded Microsoft. Larry Page and Sergey Brin founded the Google Corporation. William Proctor and James Gamble founded the Proctor and Gamble Corporation. David T. Abercrombie and Ezra Fitch founded the Abercrombie and Fitch Company. If you examine the culture of our world, you will quickly find that much of what you see around you was not built by individuals, but by people working in groups.

While this may seem obvious to you at first glance, the reality is that we may live and work in groups, but we tend to think in very solitary terms.

If we really examine our thoughts, most of us will find that we tend to keep them to ourselves. We do this for varying reasons — privacy, fear, anxiety, etc. History has shown us, however, that as with most things, the creations of humans tend to flourish in groups. If we learn to share our thoughts with others, air them out, and let them be nourished and fed by outside input, something wonderful happens. We open ourselves to a menu of possibilities that, on our own, we may not have been able to conceive.

Take the example of Linda. On her own, she had been able to create a successful life, but she was not happy with it. She wanted more. Her own best efforts could only get her so far. When she added the efforts of her friend Lysandra, well, the rest is, shall we say, history. As humans, even though we live in groups, we tend to keep our thoughts and dreams to ourselves. We fear that degree of sharing with others. Occasionally, we may open up to someone very close, but even then we hold back for fear of attack. There is some need to protect ourselves from the potential intrusion and attack of others. This too is part of our existence as humans. We do attack each other; we hurt each. But as we saw with my client in the last chapter, those too are events that we bring to the table.

If we examine the idea that life is an exercise in the creation of a menu of possibilities, we soon realize that those possibilities are greatly expanded by the inclusion of like-minded individuals who bring something to the table. Everyone is given the same possibilities, but not everyone is given the same plate of choices. By adding your menu of choices to those of others, we increase the likelihood that we will receive the happy and prosperous events in life about which we dream.

THE JOKE'S ON YOU by Phil Ryder & **YOU**

"The truth is, I don't know why I crossed the road. I was drunk, and it seemed like a good idea."
- Spencer Shellman • Santa Fe, NM

Insight Number Four

Remember to empty your cup once in a while.

James Barnett lived in a town called Ellerbe, North Carolina. The population was 1,021 at the 2000 census. It is perhaps best known as the one-time home of professional wrestler André the Giant, who operated a nearby ranch/farm in his spare time and retirement. According to the United States Census Bureau, the town has a total area of 1.5 square miles.

In his spare time, James often walked every square inch of this small town. He was born in 1916 in a small cabin on the west side of town, went to the elementary school in mid-town, and, as a child, he worked the tobacco fields that bordered the outskirts of the city. James worked for 30 years as a janitor in a furniture plant in a nearby town. He attended Sidney Grove Baptist Church, one of the 12 churches that graced the small plot of land that he called home.

He was married to his childhood sweetheart, Lucinda Barnett, and they had one child together, Mary Barnett. James never proceeded further in school than the third grade, and until his last day on earth, his signature never amounted to more than a broad and decisive X. He enjoyed sitting on his porch at the end of a long work day, sipping a cold beer, and watching the cars stream by. He enjoyed counting the number of trucks that passed his house. He seldom counted more than a couple dozen vehicles before passing out in his chair. Lucinda would wake him in time for supper, kiss him on the forehead, take his hand, and lead him into the kitchen.

His life was simple, unencumbered, and, for the most part, serene. James Barnett had mastered the art of simplicity and harmony in life. He never cursed, he never got into fights with others, and, for the most part, he lived his life in quiet celebration of the things that he could do for himself and his family. James Barnett was my grandfather, and he was the only father figure that I had in my life. Oddly enough, we never really spent that much time talking. Our relationship consisted primarily of me helping him to chop wood, work the small farm that he kept near the house, and helping him with the banking and business transactions that he needed to complete in town. My father walked away from my siblings and I when we were very young, and my grandfather, my mother's father, took us in.

My grandfather taught me how to drive, how to shoot a gun, how to shake a man's hand, how to take care of my family, and how to love the Creator with all my heart. After my grandmother passed in 1985, he lived alone in the house that they had built more than thirty years before. He continued to sit on the porch, count trucks, and fall asleep as the sun set over the Chinaberry trees that he had planted in the front yard. At least now, he didn't have to hide the beer that he loved to sip on as he rocked in his favorite chair.

My grandmother was no longer there to cook for him or lead him back into the house, but he learned to cook the meals that he liked on his own. When I visited home, I sat with him on the porch, often for hours staring at the highway, saying nothing. I always brought him a six pack of beer from the local store, and he appreciated that I remembered his favorite brand. I made it a point to visit him every time that I went home. He was not much for talking on the phone, and he did not like buses, airplanes, or trains. Since moving to Arizona, I realized that the only way that I would ever see him on any kind of a regular basis would be to visit him in Ellerbe once a year.

As my medical practice in Arizona grew, I purchased a small clinic facility in Tempe Arizona. Directly across the street from the building was a large nursing care facility for which I often provided psychiatric consultations. I suppose the care and love that I received from my grandparents had carved out a special place in my heart for the elderly. On many occasions, I visited my clients not so much as a psychiatrist, but simply because I liked seeing them and staying in touch. I met their families, their pets, their spouses, and their friends. Sometimes, we would just sit and watch television together or listen to music. Most of the time, I only had a few minutes to sit with my clients in the home. I often promised to return and spend more time, but as my practice grew, time became a rare and precious commodity.

My grandfather died in 1995. He passed away in his sleep, quietly, without pain. He had never been sick a day in his life. Ironically, I had very recently lost a wonderful older resident in the nursing facility whom I had come to like very much. She was Flemish by birth, and had been the wife of a wealthy European Ambassador before she retired to Arizona. After her husband died, she moved into the retirement facility and quickly made friends with a number of the residents. The staff called me in to help her with insomnia. Mrs. Van Damme was a well-educated, erudite, and wonderfully bright lady who smiled easily and loved to hug. When I first met her, she smiled at me and said;

"I have never touched a black man before, would you mind if I touched your face?"

I could not refuse such a humble and touching offer. From that moment on, we became friends. As I got to know her, I often thought that she and my grandfather would get along well. Even though he was about as far afield from her life as one could get, their warmth, caring, and ease of life seemed to bond them in my psyche. They died within days of each other. Even though they had never met, their lives had intersected in my heart.

The last time that I sat with both of them, they each gave me the same piece of advice. I will never forget their words. As a matter of fact, their words led me to insight number four:

Insight Number Four

Remember to empty your cup once in a while.

Both Mrs. Van Damme and my grandfather James Barnett had reminded me to sit with the people whom I love while holding hands. As simple as that advice was, when they passed, it hit me like a ton of bricks. I remembered that my grandfather liked to hold my hand as we sat on the porch and counted the trucks on the freeway. Mrs. Van Damme and I used to sit and hold hands as she listened to classical music on the public radio station. As I mourned the loss of these two precious souls, I contemplated the significance of those quiet, often unassuming moments. In my busy life, I realized that I didn't sit still very often, and when I did, I seldom took the time to do something as simple as holding another's hand.

Contemplating the concept even further, I realized that I spent very little time emptying the cup of my life at all. It seemed that I always found time to do the hundred-odd things that always filled my plate. I was a good doctor; I took care of my clients. I raised my children, I was a good husband, and I did all the things in my life that one was expected to do as a dutiful doctor, husband, and father. However, I came to realize as I laid those wonderful souls to rest, that I almost never spent more than a few minutes just enjoying the beauty of the moment. I never just held my wife's hand without watching TV, or doing a number of other things that we do while spinning through life together. I always found time to do several things at once.

In truth, I never really fully emptied my cup enough to enjoy the simple harmony of the moment.

I often held my daughter's hand when she felt sick, or hugged my son after a long day. My wife and I held hands while we watched television, and sometimes we would hold hands while we sat in the car. But I realized, even with all of these good, attentive moments of endearment, that I never really let go of the world around me long enough to fully appreciate the beauty of simply being with another person. My cup, as it were, was always full.

I wanted to stay well read. I wanted to stay in shape. I wanted to be well traveled. I wanted to see the best movies, the best plays, and listen to the best music. I wanted to build my practice, meet my financial goals, and be the best father and husband that I could be. In short, I had become adept at keeping the cup of my life full to the brim. I did not ever really stop to think about the fact that, at some point, I was going to lose all of those things. At some point, my life in this world would stop, and I would have to let go of all of those things that had filled my cup. In the same way that my grandfather and Mrs. Van Damme had slipped away, I too would slip away from this world. As a matter of fact, so too would everyone whom I'd ever met.

The process of emptying my cup would, at some point, be done for me, whether I wanted it done or not. Those two wonderful souls had given me a precious gift before leaving this world. The insight that they left me had given way to a sense of peace and harmony that remains with me to this day.

The cup of life has the capacity to fill itself each day with a myriad of tasks, both big and small, that we struggle to complete as best we can before we sleep. The reality is, however, that we can never really get it all done. No matter how hard we try, something remains undone at the end of the day.

Those little undone tasks consume the waking and sleeping moments of our lives and, without realizing it, we often surrender to worry and anxiety the serenity and peace that we truly deserve.

If we choose, we can let go of that cup and fully empty it at any moment that we choose. In a moment, we can choose to contemplate the silence of togetherness, the beauty of sharing life with another. Let me suggest a few methods that you can use to gradually learn to empty your cup:

1. Take twenty minutes a day to sit, close your eyes, and do nothing. You don't have to count your breaths, say a mantra, or visualize anything. These minutes are yours. Allow your mind to drift for this special space in time. Try to incorporate doing this each day no matter how busy your day becomes.

2. Share your twenty quiet minutes with a friend or loved one. If you like, hold their hands while you share this time. Let your minds drift together. Try not to talk. Remember to smile.

3. Take two hours each week to do something that you absolutely love. Write out a list of things that you like to do. I mean truly, absolutely like to do. Make an exhaustive search inside your psyche for those things that ignite your passion. Then, clear two hours once weekly to indulge yourself in one or more of the items on your list. You will come to find that these times will become some of the most precious and special times of your life.

I flew back home to pay my respects to my grandfather after he passed. I sat alone with him in the funeral home, and reminisced about the times that we had spent together. During those times, it seems that words are never sufficient. It always seems that we wished that we had more moments to spend.

As I looked at my grandfather, he seemed to be very much at peace. I knew that those moments that I shared with him would be our last. I had a strong belief in the afterlife; I believe that all of us continue in some form or fashion after leaving this world.

I thought about the peace and security that he had given me as a boy when he took us in. I thought about the strength and courage that I drew from him as I grew. I thought about the days that we sat on the porch and counted trucks. After an hour or so, I made myself get up and say goodbye to James Barnett. Before I left, I slipped a five dollar bill in his coat pocket. No one would ever find it, and if they did, they would not know why it had been placed there. Wherever he was going, I was sure that he would need money for his favorite beer. The next six pack that my grandfather had would be on me.

Insight Number Five

Your innermost thoughts are unique to the universe.

In his book *Quantum Healing*, Dr. Deepak Chopra reported an interesting research study that concluded the following: the average person thinks approximately 65,000 thoughts per day. The study also went on to conclude that of these 65,000 thoughts, about 95% are exactly the same thoughts that passed through the minds of these people the day before. It would appear that we spend a lot of time thinking the same mundane ideas, thoughts, and memories, and arriving at the same conclusions over and over. These thoughts take up our capacity to use the mind, intellect, and brain in new and creative pursuits. They also prevent us from developing clear powerful thoughts that are unique in our consciousness.

A recent Harvard University study shows that people spend nearly half of their waking hours daydreaming, and not thinking about what they are actually doing. Moreover, the study reports that mind wandering is a sign of unhappiness. The study, published in the journal *Science*, surveyed the thoughts and moods of over 2,200 volunteers.

The participants downloaded an iPhone app and sent more than 250,000 messages during the day and night. Researchers Matthew Killingsworth and Daniel Gilbert conclude that most of us are in another world for more than 46 per cent of our waking hours, and this means that we are unhappy: "A human mind is a wandering mind, and a wandering mind is an unhappy mind," they said.

Your thoughts have a powerful effect on you. They affect your attitude, your physiology, and your motivation to act. Your negative thoughts actually control your behavior. They can make you stutter, spill things, forget your lines, or breathe shallowly.

Research indicates that the average person talks to him/herself about 55,000 words per day. According to psychological researchers, it is 77% negative; things such as... "I shouldn't have said that," "They don't like me," "I don't like the way my hair looks today," "I can't dance," "I'll never be a good skater," "I'm not a speaker," "I'll never lose this weight," "I can't ever seem to get organized," "I'm always late" etc.

We also know from lie detector tests that your body reacts to your thoughts. These physiological changes, such as heart rate and breathing rate, occur when you're lying, but also in reaction to every thought that you think. Every cell in your body is affected by every thought that you have.

As a psychiatrist, my main work is the business of helping people to unravel the persistent negative self-talk that is often associated with mental and emotional illness. Most people don't realize just how much they are held hostage by the negative nature of their own thoughts. The fact that we regularly allow our minds to wander aimlessly through a dense forest of disconnected thoughts and dreams should be alarming. However, that thought is intimately connected to the insight that I would like to share in this chapter.

The human mind is a powerhouse of information, knowledge, and insight. Let us analyze some facts for a moment. If the average person thinks 65,000 separate thoughts in a single day, then over the course of one month, that same person will have generated over 1,950,000 individual thoughts. In one year, a single individual will have generated more than 23,400,000 thoughts. During the course of an 80-year lifetime, a person could generate more than 1,872,000,000 thoughts. That is almost two billion thoughts generated from the mind of the average individual!

Research shows that most of our thoughts are negative, 77% of them to be exact. But research also shows that 23% of our thoughts are positive and constructive in nature. So, if we analyze the number of thoughts generated by an average person in one lifetime, 1,872,000,000, and extract the number of them that are positive, we come up with more than 430,560,000 thoughts in the course of a lifetime. That is close to half a billion positive constructive thoughts that are generated by a single person. Now let's get to the insight.

If we examine the 23% of our thoughts that are positive and constructive, and then look at the number of them that happen in a single day, we find that we generate more than 14,950 happy, positive thoughts per day. Thomas Edison once said that genius is 99% perspiration and 1% inspiration. Just for the sake of discussion, let us accept this statement as an accurate reflection of the condition of our thoughts. If only one percent of those happy, positive thoughts are insightful, life-changing, and, in a word, brilliant, then each one of us has almost 150 of them per day! Each of us has more than half a dozen brilliant life-changing thoughts every hour of every day. More importantly, those brilliant life-changing thoughts are unique to each of us. When I pondered these numbers, I came to the next insight.

Insight Number Five

Your innermost thoughts are unique to the universe.

As you think about these numbers for a moment, a quick and certain response is sure to leap into your thoughts:

Why don't I hear these "brilliant" ideas if I have so many of them? The reality is that beneath the layers of negative self-talk, anxiety-ridden responses, fear-based conditioned reactions, meaningless daydreams, and other time-consuming distractions that we create for ourselves, lies a powerful oasis of potentially life-changing thought generated by our own minds. As humans, we are conditioned to ignore the positive, life-changing energies around us. The media, politics, world events, family dynamics, work, and a host of other energy-consuming events tend to push us to focus on the aspects of life that are negative and "real". Most of the time, we tend to ignore our thoughts and dreams. This unfortunate reality tends to lead us to focus on the negative energies around us, and then on the emotions that resonate with our surroundings. As research shows, those emotions tend toward melancholy, apathy, and unhappiness.

The unique, powerful, and brilliant thoughts that each of us generates each day are relegated primarily to the subconscious areas of the mind. Once they enter into the subconscious, most of us never see them again. Think about this for a moment: one clear, powerful, brilliant thought could lead you to a life of health, happiness, and prosperity. You might ask, what would such a thought look like? I wouldn't recognize one if it hit me in the face. How can I take advantage of those thoughts when they come up? Good questions!

First, let us examine the anatomy of a happy, life-changing thought. Since you have hundreds of them this year alone, you might want to pay close attention.

1. Life-changing thoughts are clear, concise, and to the point.

Most of the energy that we experience as thought tends to be loud, repetitive, and cluttered. Real work is required to make sense of what goes on in our heads. That is why daydreaming is so tempting to most of us. It gives us a break from the work of thinking. Life-changing thoughts are clear, simple, and concise energies that do not require a great deal of our mental power. As a matter of fact, when they arise, they tend to be empowering and life-affirming.

2. Positive, life-changing thoughts are quiet and repetitive.

Contrary to what you might believe, the most positive life-changing thoughts are quiet and repetitive. In other words, we tend to ignore them because they do not make themselves heard above the din of the negative self-chatter that we spend so much time creating. The quiet nature of these thoughts tends to make them uniquely difficult to gather and harvest.

3. Brilliant, happy thoughts tend to happen when we are in stimulating happy environments.

Thoughts are energies. The energy with which we surround ourselves tends to cause patterns of energy within the mind that we accept and recognize as our usual thought patterns. Brilliant, happy thoughts are stimulated by happy, harmonious, and brilliant energies in our environment. Have you ever noticed how you tend to feel better around some people and lousy around others? The reality is, some people have the ability to stimulate brilliant, happy thoughts in others just by their presence. You may find these people in all walks of life if you look for them. Pay attention to the people who make you feel happy and smart. Gather as many of them into your life as you can. They are true blessings from the Creator.

4. Brilliant, happy thoughts seem strange and unusual when they first appear in consciousness.

The nature of the average human mind is negative. Unfortunately, that is how most of us are wired. We can rise above those energies with work, focus, and discipline, but as we do, we find that we need to apply continuous pressure and force to maintain a positive, happy outlook on life. Try it sometimes, you will see what I mean. When brilliant, happy thoughts occur, we will tend not to recognize them. They will be rare, unusual, and different from the usual milieu of thought energies that we entertain during the course of a day. Their quiet unassuming nature does not help the matter very much. Humans are creatures of habit. We tend not to like change. We tend to like things to stay very much the same each and every day. The same is true of our thoughts. We don't like new and unusual thoughts very much as a race. History has shown that new thoughts and ideas are often met with resistance and violence.

This violence and resistance is created by the thought energy generated by our negative self-talk. Negative thought energy is just that — negative. Since that energy comprises more than 77% of our mental mass, we tend to use it a great deal in response to the world around us. The quiet and novel energy structure of positive, happy thoughts tends to make them easy targets for the bullying nature of negative thoughts. Recognize this within yourself. Resist the temptation to give in to the skeptical bullying nature of your negative thoughts. Listen to yourself think from time to time. You will find that you are a far more interesting person for doing so.

5. Life-changing thoughts arise from life events that are projected from the deepest levels of consciousness.

Life happens to us and around us each day. Sometimes, when the events of life become intense and threatening, the universe sends us positive, life-changing thoughts as a way of battling the storm. When life is most challenging, the mind tends to become more open. The open nature of the mind during this time is a rare and golden opportunity for you. During this time, you can often hear and understand the greatest and most insightful thoughts given to you by the Creator. These insights are important gifts that cannot only help you to rise above the pain and struggle that define the moment, but also grant you the ability to avoid similar situations in the future through the wisdom that they impart.

6. The greatest of these life-changing, brilliant thoughts are unique to you. No one else will ever have them. Ever.

One of the most important insights into the nature of life-changing, brilliant thoughts is the fact that many of them are unique to you. Many people do not see themselves as bright or deserving of the better gifts of life. Many people easily engage in negative self-talk because it is a reflection of the lives to which they have become accustomed. In reality, the Creator gives us all thousands of brilliant, creative, and potentially life-changing thoughts on a regular basis. More importantly, and perhaps miraculously, he regularly gives each of us our own special brilliant thoughts. These thoughts are unique to each of us and no one else will ever have them.

<u>Others may have similar thoughts, but no one will ever have exactly the same unique and powerful thoughts granted to you by the universe.</u>

So what are some of the greatest thoughts and ideas that mankind has ever conceived? Amazingly, many of the ideas that have pushed mankind forward have arisen from the world of thought and consciousness. Let's take a look at some of the most powerful creations that stem from the unique world of thought.

The Printing Press

The Theory of Evolution

The Telephone

The Airplane

Television

The Theory of Relativity

The Computer

Newtonian Physics, Calculus, and the Theory of Gravity

Musical Compositions

Books

The Discovery of DNA

Modern Democracy

Socialism and Marxism

Chocolate Chip Ice Cream (my personal favorite)

If you examine the above list closely, you will quickly notice that life as we know it would not be possible without the vast majority of the items listed. When Alexander Graham Bell invented the telephone, he could never have envisioned the power and grandeur of the effect that his work would have on the course of human history. When Albert Einstein wrote the *Theory of Relativity*, he could not have foreseen the far-reaching effects that his work would have on the world of science. The list that I could have placed here could ostensibly take up pages and pages, but you get the point.

How does one learn to get in touch with the important, life-changing thoughts with which we are gifted on a daily basis?

Albert Einstein was one of the greatest thinkers of all time. His ideas changed our view of reality in more ways than almost any other human being. I admire his thought process and the way that he arrived at changes in his thinking patterns. Albert Einstein would start with simply the barest of axioms—the things he was absolutely sure were true—and didn't accept anything else. When he followed these axioms to their natural conclusions, he knew that they were right—no matter how improbable—, or even if they contradicted standard dogma. He was not afraid to question the traditional ways of thinking that pervaded physics. He questioned standard beliefs because they contradicted theories that he had carefully worked out based on a few truths in which he had full faith. He didn't question willy-nilly; he simply refused to accept theories that weren't borne out by work that he had done himself.

Most of us are defined by thoughts created by ideas that we have become accustomed to embracing on a repetitive basis. For many people, these amalgamations of ideas and thoughts define who they are in a very dogmatic manner. In order to hear the whispers of greatness that the universe gives us each day, we must learn a new skill. In order to acquire this skill, we must perform one very important act.

A. **Write down the ten most important beliefs that you hold about yourself and the world around you. Now, engage in a very vigorous debate process with yourself as to why you hold on to these "truths" so tightly. Use the Internet. Do some research about the ideas. Ask people whom you respect what they think. <u>Do your best to deconstruct the ideas.</u> If they hold up to your best scrutiny and investigation, then the ideas are worth preserving. If they do**

**not hold up to your scrutiny, then you
have evolved your thinking to the next
highest level. Evolution is the point. If
we do not evolve, then happiness
becomes impossible. Personal evolution
and happiness are linked at a very deep
level.**

When it comes to drawing inspiration from
Albert Einstein, it doesn't take, well, an
Einstein, to figure out that his habits are
worth emulating. But it's the processes
behind those habits that can truly propel a
person to new heights. He went beyond just
questioning the establishment, creating
entirely new ways to do so. He relished the
chance to swim upstream because he knew
that he was right; not out of arrogance or
overconfidence, but because he had done
the work. In the end, he didn't just resist the
consensus — he created a whole new one.

Another way to create a new paradigm for
yourself by discovering your inner happy
oasis is meditation. Those still quiet thoughts
that define our greatest potential will not be

heard through the din of our daily lives. The best way to get in touch with those thoughts and ideas is through meditation. Quite simply, meditation is the best way to identify the still quiet thoughts that grace our unique neural pathways. Meditation is free, quick, and very easy to do. Meditation has been shown to have a large number of benefits. A few of the physical benefits are that it:

1- Lowers oxygen consumption
2- Decreases respiratory rate
3- Increases blood flow and slows the heart rate
4- Increases exercise tolerance
5- Leads to a deeper level of physical relaxation
6- Reduces high blood pressure
7- Reduces anxiety attacks by lowering the levels of blood lactate
8- Decreases muscle tension
9- Helps with chronic diseases such as allergies, arthritis etc.
10- Reduces Pre-menstrual Syndrome symptoms.
11- Helps with post-operative healing

12- Enhances the immune system

13- Reduces the activity of viruses and emotional distress

14- Enhances energy, strength, and vigor

15- Helps with weight loss

16- Reduction of free radicals, less tissue damage

17- Higher skin resistance

18- Drop in cholesterol levels, lowers risk of cardiovascular disease

19- Improves air flow to the lungs resulting in easier breathing

20- Decreases the aging process.

21- Increases levels of DHEAS (Dehydroepiandrosterone)

22- Prevents, slows, or controls pain associated with chronic diseases

23- Makes you sweat less

24- Cures headaches and migraines

25- Promotes orderliness of brain functioning

26- Reduces need for medical care

27- Reduces wasted energy

28- Increases inclination to participate in sports and other activities

29- Provides significant relief from asthma

30- Improves performance in athletic events

31- Normalizes ideal weight

32- Harmonizes the endocrine system

33- Relaxes the nervous system

34- Produces lasting and beneficial changes in brain electrical activity.

All of the above benefits have been documented by hundreds of sound clinical studies. Most people believe that meditation can help the body, but they are unaware of its psychological benefits. These include the following:

35- Builds self-confidence.

36- Increases serotonin levels, influences mood and behavior.

37- Resolves phobias and fears

38- Helps to control one's own thoughts

39- Helps with focus and concentration

40- Increases creativity

41- Increases brain wave coherence

42- Improves learning ability and memory

43- Increases feelings of vitality and rejuvenation

44- Increases emotional stability

45- improves relationships

46- Decelerates aging of the mind

47- Facilitates removal of bad habits

48- Develops intuition

49- Increases productivity

50- Improves relations at home and at work

51- Enables one to see the larger picture in a given situation

52- Helps one to ignore petty issues

53- Increases the ability to solve complex problems

54- Purifies one's character

55- Develops will power

56- Facilitates greater communication between the two brain hemispheres

57- Enhances the ability to react more quickly and more effectively to a stressful event

58- Increases one's perceptual ability and motor performance

59- Results in higher intelligence growth rate

60- Increases job satisfaction

61- Increases the capacity for intimate contact with loved ones

62- Decreases potential mental illness

63- Facilitates better, more sociable behavior

64- Reduces aggressiveness

65- Helps with quitting smoking, alcohol addiction

66- Reduces dependency on drugs, pills, and pharmaceuticals

67- Reduces need for sleep to recover from sleep deprivation

68- Requires less time to fall asleep, helps to cure insomnia

69- Increases sense of responsibility

70- Reduces road rage

71- Decreases restless thinking

72- Decreases tendency to worry

73- Increases listening skills and empathy

74- Helps one to make more accurate judgments

75- Facilitates greater tolerance

76- Enables composure to act in considered and constructive ways

77- Develops a stable, more balanced personality

78- Develops emotional maturity.

Meditation is easy to learn. The basic method that I teach is as follows:

Sit upright in a chair with your back straight.

Close your eyes, rest both feet flat on the floor.

Breathe in through your nose and out through your mouth.

Place your hands flat on your thighs.

Allow your mind to follow your breath in through your nose and out through your mouth. If your mind wanders, do not fight with it. Simply refocus your thoughts on your breathing. Allow the interrupting thought to pass by like a cloud in the sky.

Do this for 20 minutes per day. For best result, do not use music, mantras, or noise of any kind while you are learning the basics. As you progress, you may add those tools to your meditation.

After your meditation, write down any thoughts that you recall. With time, you will begin to coup the above benefits from your simple 20-minute practice. With luck, you will also begin to capture some of those elusive yet brilliant thoughts that the universe whispers into your ear each and every day. Remember, they are yours and yours alone. No one else will ever have them in the way that you do. Listen to yourself.

THE JOKE'S ON YOU by Phil Ryder & **YOU**

© 2004 Phil Ryder · www.thefunnypages.com

The USA's TV courtroom craze finally hits the land down under. Meet **Judge Joey.** - clem · Unknown

Insight Number Six

As you evolve, your world will evolve around you.

Jimmy Earl was 12 years old when we completed our first session. He was a small boy for his age, and he rarely looked up at me as he spoke. Jimmy loved sports, and he never missed a Lakers game or a chance to see the Diamondbacks play in the new Bank One ballpark that the city had just completed downtown. Two days before I met him, Jimmy ran away from home and left a note on his parents' dresser. The note explained that he wanted to kill himself. He planned to leave his home, walk into a bad neighborhood, and let himself be attacked by a gang. To ensure that his plan would be successful, he had taken the liberty of stealing some money from his father's wallet. He was going to flash the cash as flamboyantly as possible. Jimmy had not told his parents anything about his plan prior to running away. They did not understand the sudden change of emotion in their otherwise healthy and stable young Jimmy.

When they discovered the note, his parents immediately called the police. The Earls lived in an affluent Ahwatukee Phoenix neighborhood. However, should he choose to, they realized that Jimmy could very easily catch a ride to one of the nearby south side districts filled with gangs. Fortunately, Jimmy had chosen to leave early in the morning, just before rush hour. The police found him eating an ice cream in a McDonald's three miles away from the family home.

Jimmy's mother was a close friend of my receptionist. As luck would have it, my first appointment had been canceled the night before, and I was left with an opening. Jimmy was the first client that I saw that day.

As he sat across from me, he refused to say anything for several minutes. In a 45-minute session, time was always precious. I had to figure out some way to breach his defenses.

"How was the ice cream, young man?"

Jimmy looked up and stared blankly at me. A thin smile brushed across his face.

"I heard that you had some this morning. Did you get the chocolate coating?"

Jimmy shook his head slowly. Despite himself, he looked up at me again and laughed.

"You are good, Doctor. You asked me about the one thing that has absolutely nothing to do with why my parents brought me here."

"What can I say, I like ice cream."

"Okay, you win...they laughed at me...all of them."

"Who laughed at you?"

Jimmy took his shoes off, placed them neatly by his feet, and curled up on the couch. He pulled the velvet-lined pillow close to his face, and buried his head. After a few moments, he took a deep breath, and removed the pillow from his head.

"The guys in gym class."

"What happened, Jimmy?"

"We started basketball last week. I really looked forward to it. You know, I really, really, like the Lakers. So every day after school, I practiced shooting, and I got really good too. I could shoot just like Kobe when I put my mind to it."

"So what happened in class?"

"It wasn't so much what happened in class as what didn't happen."

"What didn't happen?"

"Every time I touched the ball, somebody pushed me, tripped me, or knocked me down. I didn't even get a chance to shoot. Coach didn't stop them. He laughed too. I'm never going back there."

Jimmy didn't cry. He didn't look up. He simply stared at the wall. I knew that he was angry, and the emotions that he didn't express had been the fuel for his suicidal gesture. If he really wanted to kill himself, he wouldn't have stopped for ice cream. The rage that drove his gesture was still building inside him.

 So why did you stop for ice cream? I read your note."

"Look, would you stop it with the ice cream already? I was hungry, alright? I didn't stop for breakfast before I left the house."

"What did you do this morning before you left, besides writing that note?"

Jimmy sat up, placed his feet on the floor, and scratched the curly black locks of hair. He was probably trying to find a way to avoid my question.

"If you must know, I didn't sleep much last night. I just sat there thinking about where I would go. I knew gym class was first period and I just couldn't face them. They would just laugh at me and push me around again."

"Did you tell your parents what happened last week?"

"Well, yea, no....I don't know. I know what they would say anyway. They would say stand up for yourself. If one of them tries to hit you, hit back and they will leave you alone. Look at me, do you think anybody's gonna be scared of a runt?"

"Is that what you think you are?"

"I'm 4'9" and 85 pounds soaking wet. I am the smallest guy in my class. They push me around all the time. What kinda basketball player can I be if I can't even get a shot off?"

Jimmy had a point. He was very small for his age. He would never stand a chance against boys his age who were bigger, stronger, and more aggressive. We talked about basketball, his favorite teams, his favorite moves, and his dreams about playing in the NBA one day.

As we talked, I realized that this child possessed a burning passion for the sport. He was not likely to let it go, though his emotional coping skills would need a lot of work. I had to find a way to help him navigate the unfair waters within which life had set him adrift.

"I want you to realize two things about yourself, Jimmy. One, you will grow up. You are still very young and nature is not quite done with you. You may be small now, but that will not always be the case."

"How do you know that?"

"How tall is your Dad?"

"You saw him, he is about 6'2"."

"How tall is your grandfather?"

"'Bout the same, maybe a little taller? What does that have to do with me?"

"Jimmy, in all likelihood, you are going to be that height one day. Give yourself some time. Not only will you be taller, but you will be bigger, just like your parents. That's called genetics, kind of a law of nature."

"I know what genetics is, Doctor Gibson. You said two things; what is this second great realization that you want to share with me?"

Sometimes, I just loved teenagers.

"Can you dribble?"

"What do you mean? Of course I can dribble."

"Show me."

I kept a basketball in the closet behind the front desk in my office. There were some courts next to my parking space, and from time to time, I used the courts as a way of breaking the ice between myself and my clients. I threw Jimmy the ball and asked him to follow me.

I winked at his parents as we walked out of the office and motioned for them to follow me. Once we reached the courts, I asked them to sit on the bleachers and remain quiet. Jimmy and I headed for the goals. I threw him the ball.

"So you wanna play me, is that it? You must be a hundred years old, guy....I'll spot you."

Jimmy immediately dribbled around the middle of the court, and headed in for a layup. He had perfect form. I was amazed at his balance and dexterity.

Jimmy was an entirely different person on the court. He was animated, happy, and more energized than I thought possible for someone who had just written a suicide note.

"Now, show me your dribbling."

Jimmy chased the ball down, picked it up, and began to dribble. First with his right hand, and then with his left. Slowly at first, but he gradually began to pick up speed.

"I want you to dribble from one end of the court to the other, first with the right hand, then the left, for the next five minutes."

"That's no fun, you can't score doing that?!"

"Yes and no. You see, Jimmy, if you dribble well enough, they will never catch you. If they can't catch you, they can't trip you, push you down, or try to hurt you. Once you get away from them, you can do whatever you like with the ball."

Jimmy paused and ran his hands through his hair for a moment. Then, as quick as a flash, he tossed the ball out in front of his body, and raced down the court dribbling with his right hand. He came back up the court dribbling with his left hand. I doubt that I could run up and down the court without the ball as fast as he was dribbling.

The longer he dribbled, the faster he moved. After five minutes, I knew that my idea had taken root. He wasn't even winded.

"When you go home, Jimmy, I want you to practice dribbling for two hours every day. Set up obstacles for yourself. Dribble up and down the driveway. Dribble around the car. Dribble around your bike. Dribble with your right hand. Dribble with your left hand. Dribble behind your back. Dribble between your legs. And remember, above all, go as fast as you can and never slow down."

Jimmy looked up at me and smiled. He understood the point that I was trying to make. Our session was over, but he was already a different person than the sad young boy who had walked into my office.

One week later, I saw Jimmy again. He had been practicing just as I'd asked. We went to the court and he showed me his new moves. Indeed, he was even faster than the first time that we'd played together.

"Have you been back to gym class yet?"

"Not yet. I'm still scared."

"I have a hunch, Jimmy. If you go back to class and forget about shooting for a while, and just show them how well you can dribble, you are going to impress some people. You have a real talent for handling the ball."

"You really think so?"

"I have seen it for myself. You are a natural. No, you can't make a lot of points dribbling, but you will get to play and you will be an important member of the team."

"You mean like the point guard?"

"Exactly. And sometimes, the point does get to shoot."

"You're a funny guy, Doctor Gibson. Okay, I'll do it."

I saw Jimmy two weeks later. He had continued to practice dribbling for two hours per day. His father gave him a DVD produced by Magic Johnson that gave instructions on ball handling, dribbling, and ways to integrate a more thorough understanding of the game into moving with and without the ball.

Jimmy went back to gym class. He took the ball and dribbled for 10 minutes before anyone could catch him. The coach eventually blew his whistle and stopped him. The coach asked Jimmy to shoot a few free throws and to make some layups. Jimmy sank all of his shots. To Jimmy's surprise, the coach asked him to try out for the summer league team that he was forming.

Jimmy made the team and was a star player. He started as point guard and averaged more than 16 points, 12 assists, and 8 rebounds per game. Nature helped him out quite a bit. As he got older, he grew to be 6'3", 195 pounds. I saw Jimmy from time to time as he matured, and made it a point to attend some of his games. After his junior varsity team won the city title and he was named MVP, I made my way down to the floor to congratulate him.

Jimmy was already surrounded by his teammates, and his parents were right by his side. He spotted me in the crowd. He ran up to me and gave me a big hug. He then bent down to the floor and gave me his game ball.

"You gave me something I didn't think I had, Doctor Gibson. This ball is yours. I want you to have it."

Jimmy looked me in the eye, looked back at his parents, and nodded. Both his mother and father waved at me. I realized that he had already spoken with them about his gesture. I was deeply moved. Now I keep two basketballs in my closet.
My sessions with Jimmy led me to the next insight that I wish to share with you.

Insight Number Six

As you evolve, your world will evolve around you.

Jimmy grew up to become a star college basketball player and a successful businessman. People never pushed him around again on the court after he learned to find the strength within himself to expertly handle a basketball. Initially, his focus on the court was to shoot and score as many baskets as possible. His size, however, did not allow him to accomplish his goal in the manner that he desired. In reality, he needed to find a way to plug himself into the game in such a way that his true abilities could shine.

Jimmy evolved in his desires, and learned to delay his immediate needs long enough to discover his true inner light.

From that moment on, he was a new person. In short, Jimmy evolved and his world evolved around him. Instead of being seen as the class runt, he was seen as that kid who "*handled the ball like a fiend*".

Quantum physics teaches us that reality is, in part, shaped by our ability to focus and perceive the quantum waves of probability that shape and mold our world. In one world, Jimmy remained a sad and unhappy young man who was placed on antidepressants, gave up basketball, and eventually grew up to be a shadow of the man that he is today. In another world, Jimmy discovered the sleeping power of subtly adjusting your attitude toward your inner skill sets, and taking the time to assess, develop, and exploit those skills to improve your life.

Many of us have been attacked by the chaos and disharmony of life. These attacks can leave us bruised, hurt, and ready to give up. The reality about these attacks is, there are various solutions to them that await the flexible, industrious mind. The willingness to evolve beyond our nascent desire to quit or feel sorry for ourselves is central to discovering our true inner power. Each of us has the power to help our worlds to evolve around us. Depending on our ability to embrace all of our strengths and skills, we can learn to leap past the tendency to hold on to attempting to replicate the skills of others.

Jimmy had fixed his gaze upon becoming another Kobe Bryant. Kobe was the league's leading scorer, and one of the strongest players in the league. Jimmy saw Kobe's skills as desirable and, without realizing it, set himself up for failure. When he took the time to find Jimmy's skill on the court, his need to become Kobe vanished. He evolved into a great player, and a very happy young man. Those insights followed him into the business world. He ultimately used his newfound confidence and poise to help him to found a highly successful startup company. You'll never guess what he sells. Jimmy now owns one of the most successful gourmet ice cream companies on the west coast.

THE JOKE'S ON YOU   by Phil Ryder & **YOU**

"Self-basting...?! What kinda turkey do they think I am?"

- Sheila Moss • Nashville, TN

Insight Number Seven

When dreams speak to you, listen carefully.

The universe around us is a wonderful and fast-moving place. From the perspective of the average person, it would appear that the earth is sitting still, and that everything around us is fixed in time and space. However, nothing could be further from the truth. The solid "fixed" earth upon which we sit is actually spinning on its axis at over 1,000 miles per hour (faster than a speeding bullet). As our earth spins, it is also moving around the sun at over 67,000 miles per hour. Even at that speed, the earth requires over 365 days to travel around the sun just once.

While the earth orbits the sun, the sun is also in orbit around the Milky Way galaxy. Believe it or not, the sun moves around the

Milky Way at over 600,000 miles per hour. The sun takes the earth and all the planets in the solar system along with it for the ride as it orbits the galaxy. From our perspective, we really don't sense any of this fantastic movement. We go along with our everyday lives, living, growing, learning, aging, and ultimately dying in the way that humans have done for tens of thousands of years.

The universe around us is a fast-moving and exciting place, but once in a while, it stops and communicates with us in a most mysterious fashion.

Dreams and visions have perplexed mankind for thousands of years. Many of the greatest thinkers and philosophers of all time have struggled with the mystery of dreams and visions, only to shake their heads and stand in deeper awe of the riddle of reality. Dreams and sleep are integral aspects of the function of the human body. On average, each of us sleeps about one-third of our lives. During an eight-hour night of sleep, we typically spend about two hours per night dreaming. If a person lives to be eighty years old, he/she will have spent more than twenty-five years sleeping, and ten years of that time in a dream state.

Scientists readily admit that the sleep state is essential for life. All animals sleep, and the mechanism by which the body regulates and establishes the sleep state is a fascinating scientific discipline in its own right. Without sleep and the accompanying dream state, life as we know it cannot exist. Sleep and dreams are essential to life and, without them, the body quickly shuts down and becomes unable to function.

The universe mandates that we take time out of each day and quietly rest the body. During this time, the universe also reveals to us the mystifying reality of dreams. The dream state is a very unusual and magical time in the life of a human. Many people have reported that life-changing revelations often come to them through the aegis of the dream state. These individuals feel that during this time, the universe itself speaks to them and reveals its plans for guidance in their lives. In many cases, the dreams have led to the creation of vast fortunes, fame, and immense happiness for those who have taken the time to write them down and follow their dictates.

Paul McCartney is one of the most famous singer/songwriters of all time. According to the *Guinness Book of Records*, his Beatles song "Yesterday" (1965) has the most cover versions of any song ever written and, according to record label BMI, was performed over seven million times in the 20th century.

The tune for "Yesterday" came to Paul McCartney in a dream...

The Beatles were in London in 1965 filming *Help!* and McCartney was staying in a small attic room of his family's house on Wimpole Street. One morning, in a dream, he heard a classical string ensemble playing, and, as McCartney tells it:

"I woke up with a lovely tune in my head. I thought, 'That's great, I wonder what that is?' There was an upright piano next to me, to the right of the bed by the window. I got out of bed, sat at the piano, found G, found F sharp minor 7th -- and that leads you through then to B to E minor, and finally back to E.

It all leads forward logically. I liked the melody a lot, but because I'd dreamed it, I couldn't believe I'd written it. I thought, 'No, I've never written anything like this before.' But I had the tune, which was the most magic thing!"

Madame C.J. Walker (1867-1919) is cited by the *Guinness Book of Records* as being the first female American self-made millionaire. She was also the first member of her family to be born free.

Madame Walker founded and built a highly successful African-American cosmetic company that made her a millionaire many times over. In the 1890s, Walker was suffering from a scalp infection that caused her to lose most of her hair. She began experimenting with patented medicines and hair care products.

Then, she had a dream that solved her problems:

"He answered my prayer, for one night I had a dream, and in that dream a big, black man appeared to me and told me what to mix up in my hair. Some of the remedy was grown in Africa, but I sent for it, mixed it, put it on my scalp, and in a few weeks my hair was coming in faster than it had ever fallen out. I tried it on my friends; it helped them. I made up my mind to begin to sell it."

Walker was an entrepreneur, philanthropist, and social activist. She best sums up her rise from a childhood in the poor south to being the head of an international, multi-million dollar corporation in the following quote:

"I am a woman who came from the cotton fields of the South. From there I was promoted to the washtub. From there I was promoted to the cook kitchen. And from there I promoted myself into the business of manufacturing hair goods and preparations....I have built my own factory on my own ground."

Madame C.J. Walker built a multi-million dollar empire around hair care products during a time when African-Americans were not allowed to vote. Her empire was inspired by her response to a dream. Had she not taken the time to record the proceedings of the dream, her life may have been vastly different.

The novelist Robert Louis Stevenson (1850-1894) described dreams as occurring in "that small theater of the brain which we keep brightly lighted all night long."

Stevenson said of his now classic novel *The Strange Case of Dr. Jekyll and Mr. Hyde*, it was "conceived, written, re-written, re-re-written, and printed inside ten weeks" in 1886, and was conceived in a dream as he describes:

"For two days I went about racking my brains for a plot of any sort; and on the second night I dreamed the scene at the window, and a scene afterward split in two, in which Hyde, pursued for some crime, took the powder and underwent the change in the presence of his pursuers."

Mrs. Stevenson has related picturesquely how one night Louis cried out horror-stricken, how she woke him up and he protested, "Why did you waken me? I was dreaming a fine bogy-tale!" She also related how he appeared the next morning excitedly exclaiming, "I have got my schilling-shocker -- I have got my schilling-shocker!"

Stevenson wrote extensively about how his passion for writing interacted with his remarkable dreams and said that, from an early age, his dreams were so vivid and moving that they were more entertaining to him personally than any literature. He learned early in his life that he could dream complete stories, and that he could even go back to the same dreams on succeeding nights to give them a different ending. Later, he trained himself to remember his dreams and to dream plots for his books. As a result of his meticulous attention to the detail of his dreams, Robert Louis Stevenson is now remembered as one of the greatest writers who ever lived. He readily admits that his dreams served as fertile soil for the production of his books.

Srinivasa Ramanujan (1887-1920) was one of India's greatest mathematical geniuses. He made substantial contributions to the analytical theory of numbers, and worked on elliptical functions, continued fractions, and infinite series. In 1914, he was invited to Cambridge University by the English mathematician GH Hardy, who recognized his unconventional genius. He worked there for five years producing startling results, and proved over 3,000 theorems in his lifetime.

According to Ramanujan, inspiration and insight for his work many times came to him in his dreams...

A Hindu goddess, named Namakkal, would appear and present mathematical formulae which he would verify after waking. Such dreams often repeated themselves, and the connection with the dream world as a source for his work was constant throughout his life.

Ramanujan describes one of his dreams of mathematical discovery:

"While asleep I had an unusual experience. There was a red screen formed by flowing blood as it were. I was observing it. Suddenly a hand began to write on the screen. I became all attention. That hand wrote a number of results in elliptic integrals. They stuck to my mind. As soon as I woke up, I committed them to writing..."

Dreams carry information of many types. They often reveal unforeseen solutions to problems that vex us during the day. These solutions often seem to spring completely out of nowhere.

Jack Nicklaus is one of the greatest golfers who ever lived. However, in 1964, he went through a terrible slump, and routinely shot in the high seventies. One night, after a bad round, a solution to his problem came to him in a dream. He fully credits the dream with saving his game. After suddenly regaining top scores, he reported:

"Wednesday night I had a dream and it was about my golf swing. I was hitting them pretty good in the dream and all at once I realized I wasn't holding the club the way I've actually been holding it lately. I've been having trouble collapsing my right arm taking the club head away from the ball, but

I was doing it perfectly in my sleep. So when I came to the course yesterday morning I tried it the way I did in my dream and it worked. I shot a sixty-eight yesterday and a sixty-five today."

After I read of these dramatic examples of the power of dreams, I stumbled upon the next insight that I will share with you.

Insight Seven

When dreams speak to you, listen carefully.

There are millions of examples of the powerful, life-changing force of dreams. In my practice, I have helped thousands of clients to unravel the mysterious messages of their dreams. Often, these dreams reveal hidden treasures that help to make their lives richer, happier, and more successful. The forces that move our universe coordinate a vast number of energies that scientists are still struggling to understand.

These energies are active inside the mind and soul of every dreaming person in existence. Sometimes, these energies emerge in their own special way and speak to us. These revelations are often powerful and life changing. Our only task in relation to these moments is to listen.

Dreams are a doorway into the universal unconscious.

The intelligence that creates, maintains, and manipulates our reality is vast and unfathomable from the perspective of our human consciousness. Each day, billions of chemical reactions take place within the body that are necessary for the maintenance of life. The heart beats hundreds of thousands of times; the brain relays billions of signals; the kidneys filter liters of blood; all without the knowledge or understanding of the conscious mind. However, there is a beautiful symphony of coordination, regulation, and maintenance that carries out all these functions. Let us call this intelligence "the universal unconscious".

This universal unconscious force has the power to regulate the movement of the stars, planets, and life forms that populate this realm of existence. This force creates breathing, thought, sunlight, ocean waves, tears, flowers, stars, and everything in the universe that we can observe. This force also resides within each of us. As creations of this force, we are also privileged to be a part of its reality.

One way to understand dreams is to imagine that they are the universe's way of sitting us down and talking to us. The conversation is constant, in that each and every day, we sleep, dream, and attempt to remember the dialogue. Some people state that they do not dream, or if they do, they never remember the content.

Science has shown that each of us does indeed dream every night. Everyone who has ever been studied for sleep disorders has been shown to have a dream state. The reality of the dream state, and its impact on our waking world, is an accepted fact of life.

However, the potentially life-changing insights delivered to us by dreams are often lost in the mists of waking. How can we save more of this power for use in our waking lives? Here are some tips that might help you to recall more of your dreams.

One. As soon as you awaken in the morning, do not immediately get up. Lie in bed for a few minutes, and focus on what you can recall of your dreams. Most of our dreams happen in the last ninety minutes of sleep. This is a great time to fix them in the mind.

Two. After lying in bed for a few minutes, get up and write down what you can recall from your dreams. If you choose, you may use a digital recorder. The images and visual data from a dream are sometimes very important. Remember to write them down.

Three. Before going to sleep at night, tell yourself to remember your dreams. This positive reinforcement from the conscious mind often helps to fix the memory of the dream state in the waking brain. This fixing process is valuable in helping to preserve the often fleeting wisps of dream material that survive into morning.

Four. Ask the universe to send you a dream in response to a problem or concern. The universe is an intelligent and powerful force that is active in your life. If you allow it, the universe can help you to change your life in ways that you never considered. Don't worry about how the change happens, where the energy comes from, or how to control its movement in your life.

Releasing the mental constraints that you place on what is "possible" in your life will help the universe to help you.

Albert Einstein is known as one of the most brilliant and analytical thinkers of all time. He received a Nobel prize in physics for his scientific achievements. However, most people do not realize that Einstein attributed his success in science to the inspiration that he received from a dream.

The famous E=MC2, the equation for the Theory of Relativity, is now synonymous with the name Albert Einstein. This theory asserts, among other things, that time travel is possible when energy and mass are equivalent and transmutable.

Einstein stated that his theory was inspired by a dream in which he was hurtling down a mountainside. As he sped faster and faster, he looked to the sky and saw that the stars were altered in appearance as he approached the speed of light. He realized that as he observed the stars whizzing by, he was in the act of witnessing a profound insight about reality. His observation of the events in this dream changed the course of human history. When the universe spoke to Albert Einstein, he listened, and changed all of our lives forever.

THE JOKE'S ON YOU   by Phil Ryder & **YOU**

© 2011 Phil Ryder · www.thefunnypages.com

"Dude...! Your tank is HUGE!!"

- ROCK · Hannibal, MO

Insight Eight

Early failure often leads to success.

In the breadth of human affairs, there is nothing more common than the presence of failure. Almost everyone in this world has attempted something in life that has succeeded in creating nothing more than a total, abject, unmitigated failure. During the course of my work in psychiatry, one of the most common themes of my sessions with clients involves working through failed endeavors: failed relationships, failed jobs, poor school performance, poor health, poor sports performance, loss of income in finance and business endeavors, the list is long and varied. Every time I face these situations with clients, however, I am amazed by the tenacity of human will, strength, and force of determination.

Most of the time, we do not expect to fail in the early stages of an endeavor. Failure is not an energy form that we tend to embrace. In our early years, most of us build up a huge wall of optimism and hope regarding life. As we age, this wall is adjusted, rebuilt, and reshaped by life's responses to our best efforts. Sometimes, the response that life gives us can fill us with happiness, light, and peace. On other occasions, when life tells us that we are somehow not good enough, not smart enough, not quite up to the goals that we set for ourselves, it is easy to forget the maxim that led to the next insight.

Insight Number Eight

Early failure often leads to success.

The pursuit of happiness and success is bound to be met with failure and disappointment. The fact is, life expects us to learn from our failures and has wired the human nervous system in such a way that we are forced to learn from the past in order to survive. History has taught us that the more we fail, the greater our success. As a matter of fact, history is full of people who might never have made a success of their lives without the challenge of early resounding failure.

The Power of Failure

Winston Churchill was a great man who failed the sixth grade, and was defeated in every single election for public office until he became Prime Minister at the young age of 62.

Sir Winston Churchill took three years to complete the eighth grade because he had trouble learning English. He suffered from a speech impediment, and had great difficulty pronouncing the letter "s". It seems ironic that years later, Oxford University asked him to address its commencement exercises.

He arrived with his usual props; a cigar, a cane, and a top hat accompanied Churchill wherever he went. As Churchill approached the podium, the crowd rose in appreciative applause. With unmatched dignity, he settled the crowd, and stood confident before his admirers. Removing the cigar and carefully placing the top hat on the podium, Churchill gazed at his waiting audience. Authority rang in Churchill's voice as he shouted, "Never give up!"

Several seconds passed before he rose to his toes and repeated: "Never give up!" His words thundered in their ears. There was a deafening silence as Churchill reached for his hat and cigar, steadied himself with his cane, and left the platform. His commencement address was finished. Because Winston Churchill never gave up, he is now remembered as one of the greatest world leaders of the twentieth century.

Sir Edmund Hillary

In 1852, the Great Trigonometric Survey of India determined that Mount Everest, until then an obscure Himalayan peak, had been definitively identified as the world's highest mountain. This announcement captured the international imagination, and soon the idea of reaching the summit of the "roof of the world" was viewed as the ultimate geographic feat. Attempts to climb Everest, however, could not begin until 1921, when the forbidden kingdom of Tibet first opened its borders to outsiders.

On June 8, 1924, two members of a British expedition, George Mallory and Andrew Irvine, attempted the summit. Famous for his retort to the press—"because it's there"—when asked why he wanted to climb Everest, Mallory had already failed twice at reaching the summit. The two men were last spotted "going strong" for the top until the clouds perpetually swirling around Everest engulfed them. Then, they vanished.

Mallory's body was not found for another 75 years, in May 1999. No evidence was found on his body—such as a camera containing photos of the summit, or a diary entry recording their time of arrival at the summit—to clear up the mystery of whether these two Everest pioneers made it to the top before the mountain killed them.

In 1952, Edmund Hillary attempted to climb Mount Everest, but failed. A few weeks after his first failed attempt, he was asked to speak to a prestigious group in England.

Hillary walked on stage to thunderous applause. The audience showered Hillary with praise because he had attempted something that no other human had ever completed. However, Edmund Hillary saw himself as a complete failure. As the applause died, he backed away from the microphone and walked to the edge of the platform.

He paused for a moment and turned to look at a picture of Mount Everest that hung in the background. He made a fist and pointed at the picture of the mountain. He said in a loud voice, "Mount Everest, you beat me the first time, but I'll beat you the next time because you've grown all you are going to grow... but I'm still growing!"

He tried again in 1953. On May 29, 1953, he succeeded in reaching the summit of the highest mountain known to man. He was knighted for his efforts. Sir Edmund Hillary is now remembered as one of the greatest explorers of all time.

Abraham Lincoln

As a young man, Abraham Lincoln went to war a captain and returned a private. Afterwards, he was a failure as a businessman. As a lawyer in Springfield, he was too impractical and temperamental to be a success. He turned to politics and was defeated in his first try for the legislature, again defeated in his first attempt to be nominated for congress, defeated in his application to be commissioner of the General Land Office, defeated in the senatorial election of 1854, defeated in his efforts for the vice presidency in 1856, and defeated in the senatorial election of 1858.

At about that time, he wrote in a letter to a friend, "I am now the most miserable man living. If what I feel were equally distributed to the whole human family, there would not be one cheerful face on the earth."

Following his 1858 defeat, battling bouts of depression, self-doubt, and lack of confidence, Abraham Lincoln pulled himself together and ran for President of the United States. Despite having lost numerous elections, failing at business, military service, and the practice of law, Lincoln felt that he could win the election and provide the kind of leadership that the country needed at its most crucial hour.

On November 6, 1860, despite all odds, Abraham Lincoln was elected as the 16th President of the United States. He was also the very first Republican ever to be elected president. He received 180 of 303 possible electoral votes, and 40 percent of the popular vote. After leading the United States through the most divisive and turbulent war of its young history, on

November 8, 1864, Abraham Lincoln was re-elected as President, defeating Democrat George B. McClellan. Lincoln received 212 of 233 electoral votes, and 55 percent of the popular vote. He is now remembered as one of our greatest presidents.

Marilyn Monroe

Norma Jean Baker, better known as Marilyn Monroe, experienced a disrupted, loveless childhood that included two years at an orphanage. When Norma Jean, born on June 1, 1926, in Los Angeles, California, was seven years old, her mother, Gladys (Monroe) Baker Mortenson, was hospitalized after being diagnosed with paranoid schizophrenia, a severe mental condition. Norma was left in a series of foster homes and the Los Angeles Orphans' Home Society. The constant move from one foster home to another resulted in Norma's "sketchy" educational background.

After Norma's sixteenth birthday, her foster parents had to move from California. To avoid an orphanage or a new foster home, Norma chose to get married. On June 19, 1942, Norma married James Dougherty, but the marriage would all but end when he joined the U.S. Merchant Marines in 1943. Though her difficult childhood and early failed marriage would make Norma Jean a strong and resilient woman, these experiences would also add to her insecurities and flaws—things that would ultimately shape her into a great tragic figure of the twentieth century.

During World War II (1939–45), a war fought between the Axis powers—Japan, Italy, and Germany—and the Allies—England, France, the Soviet Union, and the United States—, Norma Jean worked at the Radio Plane Company in Van Nuys, California; but she was soon discovered by photographers. She enrolled in a three-month modeling course, and in 1946, aware of her considerable charm and the potential that it had for a career in film, Norma obtained a divorce from Dougherty. She then headed for Hollywood, where Ben Lyon, head of casting at Twentieth Century Fox, arranged a screen test. On August 26, 1946, she signed a one hundred and twenty-five dollar per week, one-year contract with the studio. Ben Lyon was the one who suggested a new name for the young actress—Marilyn Monroe.

During Monroe's first year at Fox, she did not appear in any films, and her contract was not renewed. She was dropped by her producers because they thought that she was unattractive and couldn't act.

However, Marilyn Monroe did not give up and continued to pursue her dream. Her persistence paid off. In the spring of 1948, Columbia Pictures hired her for a small part in *Ladies of the Chorus*. In 1950, John Huston (1906–1987) cast her in *Asphalt Jungle*, a tiny part that landed her a role in *All About Eve*. She was now given a seven-year contract with Twentieth Century Fox, and appeared in *The Fireball, Let's Make*

It Legal, Love Nest, and *As Young as You Feel.*

In 1952, after an extensive publicity campaign, Monroe appeared *in Don't Bother to Knock, Full House, Clash by Night, We're Not Married, Niagara,* and *Monkey Business.* The magazine *Photoplay* termed her the "most promising actress," and she was earning top dollars for Twentieth Century Fox.

Most people would have given up on the dream of becoming something more than just another pretty face when confronted with the hurdles thrown in Marilyn's path. She held tight to her commitment to herself, and each failure only made her more determined to succeed in a field where failure was the norm. Norma Jean is now remembered as one of the greatest sex symbols of all time.

JK Rowling

Joanne Rowling often felt insecure and shy at school, even though her grades were good. Writing stories became a passion that allowed her to be herself. These stories were full of humor, funny names and characters, and magic.

In the later school years, she began to read the biographies of the great people. She admired the author Jessica Mitford, and said that the book *Hons and Rebel* had changed her life.

According to Joanne, the worst memories of her teenage years were when her mother was diagnosed with multiple sclerosis. Even though she did not fully realize at that time what it meant, it was painful for the girl to see her mother becoming slowly but steadily worse. Joanne ended her school training with high honors. She knew exactly what she wanted in her life, but had no idea where to begin.

Joanne never stopped writing; however, she never tried to submit any of her stories. She felt too insecure to take any step in the direction of her dreams.

Joanne went through a series of jobs, most of them secretarial. She found her jobs boring. The only consolation that she had was in writing. "Whatever job I had, I was always writing like crazy," she admitted later.

She wrote many short stories, and abandoned several novels. However, her work ended up in another box with all other stories, and her self-esteem declined.

After having changed several employers, she found a job as an office worker for the Manchester Chamber of Commerce. She still found her work very boring, and spent her lunchtime at a nearby pub or cafe writing her stories.

Joan's life suddenly took another turn when she was on the way to London, and her train stopped. It was some kind of mechanical problem, which required a delay of four hours. She was staring out the window, when the idea for Harry Potter appeared in her mind very clearly. "I suddenly had this basic idea of a boy who didn't know what he was," she described several years later.

She invested all her free time in writing the story, month after month, filling her files and boxes with ideas and stories. Joanne felt very happy in this world of her own; she did not even mention it to her sister nor to her parents.

At the age of forty-five, her mother died suddenly from multiple sclerosis. Joanne felt deeply the loss, mixed with a feeling of guilt and regret. Her deepest regret was that she never let her mother read her Harry Potter story.

Shortly thereafter, Joanne lost her job at the Manchester Chamber of Commerce. At that time, Harry was the only motivation that got her through.

In September 1990, Joanne decided that she would no longer look for office work. She accepted the offer of a job in Portugal, teaching English as a second language at school. For the first time, she was happy about her job, and her students were happy to be taught by her. She worked afternoons and evenings, and devoted her mornings to writing.

Her life changed when she met and fell in love with journalist Jorge Arantes. A few months later, they got married.

Joanne kept writing... Her book, which had started as a typical children's book, had become more detailed, having acquired the depth suited for adult readers. In 1993, her daughter Jessica was born. However, the newly born child did not strengthen the couple's relationship, which by then had become very stressful.

After the breakup with her husband, Joanne took a decision to return to the U.K. with her four-month-old baby Jessica.

She moved to Edinburgh, Scotland, to be near her sister Di. It was a hard time for a single mother. Due to the fact that she was not eligible for child care, Joanne was forced into unemployment and public assistance. Public assistance barely covered rent and food, and Joanne could not afford even a second-hand typewriter.

Nicolson Cafe had become her favorite place to write Harry Potter.

At what was probably the lowest period of her life, her daughter Jessica and her Harry Potter were the only inspirations. During this period, Joanne suffered from deep depression. She finally confessed to her sister about the story of Harry Potter, which Di found immediately thrilling and captivating. "It's possible if she had not laughed, I would have set the whole thing to one side," admitted Joanne, "but Di did laugh." She persuaded Joanne to take a risk and send her book to publishers. Twelve publishers rejected the book before a small London publisher finally accepted it.

Even then, the editor of Bloomsbury (the publishing company), due to his doubt about the success of the book, advised Rowling to get a day job as it was unlikely that she would make money from it.

But Rowling's belief in her work didn't sway. The book was eventually published in 1997, with a print run of 1000, five hundred of which were distributed to libraries. The Harry Potter books are now one of the biggest selling series of novels in history. Joanne is now a billionaire and one of the most sought-after speakers of all time. She is, in my opinion, one of the greatest teachers in the world. Her story is indeed a testament to the power of failure, and not giving up before you embrace the happiness that you truly desire.

Chaos, despair, and disappointment are common pitfalls that everyone has to face in life. In reality, the challenge of life is not what matters most. How we choose to face the challenge is infinitely more important. Most people seek the approval of others before pushing forward with a dream. If we do not receive that approval, it is often easy to relegate success and happiness to the far corners of our minds, or let it go altogether.

When we are young, life seems to have no boundaries. Dreams are plentiful and, at times, anything seems possible. For many people, however, emotional setbacks, failures, or loss of a loved one signal the end of the period of dreaming. The focus then becomes survival and the avoidance of failure. This is not the way of happiness.

Happiness feeds on failure and is nurtured by the inevitable success that follows true persistence.

I would like to end this chapter with a rather poignant story that I found that illustrates this point.

Dante Gabriel Rossetti, the famous 19th-century poet and artist, was once approached by an elderly man. The old fellow had some sketches and drawings that he wanted Rossetti to look at and tell him if they were any good, or if they at least showed potential talent.

Rossetti looked them over carefully. After the first few, he knew that they were worthless, showing not the least sign of artistic talent. But Rossetti was a kind man, and he told the elderly man as gently as possible that the pictures were without much value and showed little talent. He was sorry, but he could not lie to the man. The visitor was disappointed, but seemed to expect Rossetti's judgment.

He then apologized for taking up Rossetti's time, but would he just look at a few more drawings, these done by a young art student. Rossetti looked over the second batch of sketches and immediately became enthusiastic over the talent that they revealed. "These," he said, "oh, these are good. This young student has great talent. He should be given every help and encouragement in his career as an artist. He has a great future if he will work hard and stick to it."

Rossetti could see that the old fellow was deeply moved. "Who is this fine young artist?" he asked. "Your son?" "No," said the old man sadly. "It is me — 40 years ago. If only I had heard your praise then! For you see, I got discouraged and gave up — too soon."

THE JOKE'S ON YOU   by Phil Ryder & **YOU**

"Now, kids, before we have our first flight lesson, does anyone need to use the windshield?"

- T. McConnell • Averagetown, USA

Insight Nine

The hunger created by unfulfilled desire is the main cause of human unhappiness.

Bob Bannon, a friend of mine whom I had known since medical school, called me unexpectedly one day. Bob was born in New York City, and was the child of Irish immigrant parents. We met just shortly after I began medical school at Chapel Hill. Bob was part of my medical class, and always saw himself as a budding surgeon. He was 6'5" tall, handsome, and well spoken. He always had his pick of the nurses, technicians, and resident doctors on the ward when he showed up. When time permitted, Bob and I played chess and chatted about Tarheel basketball, school, and his newest female conquest.

Bob married a beautiful dermatology attending physician while he was in residency at Michigan. When he completed his training, they got married, moved to Ann Arbor, and began a family. They had two children and began to settle into what appeared to be a fairly happy, upper-middle-class life. As we talked, Bob and I caught up on each other's lives, and reminisced about the days before receding hairlines, expanding bellies, and worries about the stock market and managed care companies. After a few minutes of chatting, I asked Bob why he had called.

"I didn't know who else to turn to, Mitch. I can still hardly process it myself."

"Process what Bob? What is going on?"

"It's my wife, Mitch. Yesterday, she told me that she is having an affair."

"I'm sorry to hear that, Bob."

I could hear the sorrow and heartbreak in his voice. Bob and Terri had been together for more than ten years. I hoped that they could weather the storm that life had brought to their shores.

"You haven't heard the best part. She asked me to join them in bed."

"Join them?...You mean three-way sex...with the person that she is having an affair with?"

"That's right. Oh by the way, I forgot to mention, her name is Barbara."

"Who's Barbara?"

"The woman my wife is having an affair with."

"Okay, let me get this straight, Bob. Your wife, the mother of your children, is having an affair with a woman named Barbara. And, she wants you to join them in bed?"

"That's right. I don't know if I should kill myself or buy Viagra."

Bob's response to his situation was funny, and I desperately wanted to laugh. But from the sound of his voice, I could tell that he was dead serious. The situation, though unusual by any social standard, was not one that I had not seen before.

"I am sorry to hear about this, my friend, though it is a strange predicament for your wife to place you in. Why do you think that she asked you to join them?"

"That question, Mitch, is the reason for my call today. If you have a moment, I need to tell you a story."

At the time, I was between clients and nearing my lunch break. Just before Bob's call, I had buzzed my secretary and asked her who was next on my schedule. As luck would have it, my next client had canceled, and I found myself with thirty free minutes. "Bob, I have some time. Talk to me."

"Remember when we were in med school and we used to talk about the future, all the things we were going to do, the places we would go?"

"Yes I do. We both were quite the dreamers."

"Well, I wrote down all the things that I wanted to do and put them in a book. I called it my Book of Shadows. When I finished my residency and started to make some money, I decided to dig up that book and see just how many items on that list I could actually live out.

As luck would have it, most of them were fairly easy and straightforward. I traveled all over the world; Paris, London, Munich, Rio, Cancun, Egypt, Singapore, Bangkok, you name it. I loved it. I jumped out of airplanes, scuba dived with sharks, ate plates of puffer fish, ran with the bulls at Pamplona, and slept with every kind of woman that I ever dream about.

I made a couple of million during the Dot.com boom, and put that away for a rainy day. Marrying Terri was on my list and as you know, I checked that one off too. So now, we come to the kicker. I showed Terri my list a couple of years ago. She was the only person that I had ever dared to show it to. Mitch, I have completed everything I ever really wanted in life that I put on that list, except for the last item. Can you guess what that was?"

"Knowing you, Bob, I will guess that it had to do with sex. Oh no! You can't be serious!"

"You got it, I wanted to have a three-way with my wife and a beautiful blond coed."

"Let me guess, your wife's lover is a beautiful blonde coed?"

"Bingo."

I had been in Bob's wedding. Terri was a beautiful and sensitive woman. From my perspective, they had always been a happy and well-adjusted couple. I had not had contact with him for several years, but I did not believe that Terri could have changed that much. I wondered if she had set the whole thing up for Bob's benefit.

"Bob, I have a question. Do you think Terri is doing this for you? She did see your list. Do you think she is helping you close out your book of shadows?"

"That was the first thing I asked her."

"What did she say?"

"You are not going to believe her answer."

"Try me."

"She said, 'if I'm being honest, if you say yes, I get to kill two birds with one stone'."

"Implying that she wants to do this as much as you do..."

"Bingo. I guess that is why you went into psychiatry, Mitch. Part of me wants desperately to do this, but I think Terri might have some real desire to be with this girl without me. I am scared that if I don't do this, she might leave me. But, on the other hand, if I give in, the chaos might end our relationship."

"I understand why you called me now, Bob. This whole situation is strangling you emotionally. Even though the desire to have a three-way with your wife is on your all-time list of wants, you have found out that the unfulfilled desire is more than you bargained for."

Bob and I talked several times after that initial conversation. Ultimately, he and Terri sought out marital therapy and even included her love interest in a couple of the sessions. They separated for a brief time but eventually, they mended their relationship and are now expecting their third child.

Bob's dilemma made me think about the nature of desire, happiness, and emotional hunger in our lives. Bob had always been a driven and focused individual. Those traits were very common in all of us who made it through college, medical school, and residency; the need to succeed, achieve, and deliver upon the promises that our God-given talents had stamped upon our lives. Bob had lived out his dreams, as much as any man or woman could possibly dare. However, he was still hungry.

The situation that Bob presented was not as uncommon as you might think. To be sure, not many of us are faced with such an unusual sexual dilemma, but the thread of reality woven by the situation is very relevant to the lives of millions. What happens when you achieve everything that you've ever wanted? What happens if you don't achieve everything that you desire?

At first glance, one might surmise that very few people ever really achieve what they want in life. If you listen to the negativity in the media and the scientific community, the overwhelming majority of Americans think that they're falling behind financially, are despondent about their lives and their futures, and are desperately looking for a change.

Yet, a new Gallup poll confirms what NewsBusters, the Business & Media Institute, and parent of the Media Research Center has been saying for years: people are far happier with themselves and their lives than press members care to report.

In fact, the difference between what people feel about their immediate environment and what they think is going on outside of their sphere of influence is a stunning indictment of just how skewed the media's account of the world really is.

According to a December 6-9, 2007 Gallup poll, 84% of Americans say that they are satisfied with the way that things are going in their personal lives at this time, while 14% are dissatisfied. These results have been fairly stable since Gallup first started tracking Americans' personal life satisfaction in 1979. The percentage of Americans who say that they are satisfied with their personal lives has averaged 82% over this period, with a low of 73% in July 1979, and a high of 88% in December 2004.

Bob clearly falls into the group of Americans who report a high degree of satisfaction with life, but he still contemplated killing himself in response to his marital crisis. As a matter of fact, even though most people in the United States (and around the world) report a fairly high degree of satisfaction with their lives, the World Health Organization reports that over the last 45 years, suicide rates worldwide have increased by over 60%. Somewhere in the world, a person kills him/herself every forty seconds. If we accept suicide as an indicator of some degree of unhappiness in one's life, how can we reconcile this seeming inequity in the reporting of the emotional state of affairs in our world? How can people report such high degrees of satisfaction with life and still kill themselves at such alarming rates?

Over the years, I have treated thousands of people who have attempted suicide. During the recovery phase of their treatment, I have noted a recurring theme in the reasons for their attempts. Almost every person who I treated for this dilemma admitted that the reason that he/she attempted suicide was that he/she could not fulfill some deep-seated desire. The desires spanned the gamut of human experience.

Sometimes the need was to get out of debt. Sometimes, the client wanted to leave a relationship or a job and could find no way out. Sometimes he/she wanted to find a cure for a disease, but lost hope. Sometimes, he/she simply could not find a way to satisfy the desire to go on living another day.

When I distilled the answers down to their finest essence, I stumbled upon an insight — the ninth insight:

Insight Nine

The hunger created by unfulfilled desire is the main cause of human unhappiness.

We all have desires. Desire is one of the basic drives that propels human consciousness forward. The act of being is intimately associated with the desire to act, to feel, to achieve. None of us is immune to this basic reality. However, some of the desires that we strive to fulfill in life are destined to be unfulfilled. This, too, is a basic reality of human existence. So how can we learn to evolve beyond this seemingly endless cycle?

The concept of happiness is basic to the human condition. The Gallup Poll that I quoted earlier outlines the fact that most of us are fairly happy with our lot in life. However, when stress and chaos build in life, and we are confronted with problems that seem insurmountable, too often, we turn to drugs, alcohol, and suicide.

Too often, we allow the hunger for things that we cannot have in life to take away our ability to fully enjoy the gifts that we already have.

The Buddha taught that "All life is suffering," in the first of his Four Noble Truths. Physical illness and mental illness are suffering; not to obtain what one desires is suffering; to be united with what one dislikes or separated from what one likes is suffering. A great philosopher once said: the world is not a problem for a person with no preferences. This truth about life leads many people to seek out paths to enlightenment, meditation, and spiritual practice as a way to end the hunger.

Millions of people are drawn to Eastern spirituality and meditation for this reason. Once they identify the cause of their suffering as desire, they struggle to eliminate it from their being. A number of these people have come to work with me, wondering why their spiritual pursuits have not brought them the peace of mind that they were expecting. I have noticed that quite often, spiritual pursuits and meditation can lead to anxiety, bitterness, and unhappiness. For the most part, I have come to believe that this happens because most people are not honest about their reasons for seeking out a spiritual path in the first place.

I find that many people see the desire to evolve beyond the basic nature of human need as a sign of the evolution of consciousness. However, through therapy and working through their true feelings, a very different understanding of the concept of need and desire emerges.

Most people find that for the vast majority of their lives, they tend to diminish and fold their desires down to the smallest and most workable ratios that life will allow.

When they become more honest about their desires, a different feeling emerges. The concept of desire is interlinked with hunger; and therein lies the problem. If we learn to expand our desires and use them to help us to evolve, then we can learn to use the hunger rather than be used by it. A well-known Indian teacher, Sri Nisargadatta, once commented, "The problem is not desire. It's that your desires are too small." Opening to desire allows it to become more than just a craving for whatever the culture has conditioned us to want. Desire is a teacher: When we immerse ourselves in it without guilt, shame, or clinging, it can show us something special about our own minds that allows us to embrace life fully.

This new way of conceiving desire may be a true path to freedom for millions. Examining what we truly want without restraint or fear of ridicule often leads us to embrace the deepest aspect of self, the part of who we are that seeks in the first place; the soul.

Look at what you really want in life, and then magnify the thought. Blow it up to a proportion that you never dreamed possible. Expand upon the desire until you can no longer see the edges of what you want. Let's take Bob for instance. I believe that the root of Bob's fear with his relationship was a yearning for greater sexual freedom than his ego could allow. His wife was the first to express this need, and the confrontation shattered Bob's resistance to facing the idea within himself. His therapist suggested that they experiment with swinging as a way to resolve the conflict presented by his wife's new lover. The couple did just this for six months. Bob found that even though the experience was fun initially, his heart really didn't want to share Terri with another lover. He found that once he had thoroughly tested the limits of his hunger, he could come to terms with his need to explore his world sexually. What he needed, however, was the freedom to test those limits.

Rather than treating desire as the cause of hunger and suffering, one can choose to embrace it as a valuable and precious resource, an emotion that, if harnessed correctly, can awaken and liberate the soul for a fuller and more evolved life.

THE JOKE'S ON YOU — by Phil Ryder & **YOU**

"Look, it's mine and I want it back."
- Sher Surratt • Cleveland, OH

Conclusion

Happiness and success are states of existence that we all strive to attain. The greatest achievements in human history have been attained by those individuals who strive to elevate themselves above the everyday ebb and flow of life. This yearning to achieve is central to our search for happiness. We want to laugh, to sing, and to feel good at the end of the day as much as we might wish to do anything else.

The overall goal of this book has been to show you, the reader, a few examples of the power of an open mind. As a psychiatrist, I have seen that human optimism, and its attendant yearning for happiness, tends to fall into a long, slow, almost inevitable decline as we face the struggles of life. Most people are content with their lives, but happiness remains a goal that most only faintly hope to attain.

Happiness is an art. If you wish to practice this art, you must first decide that it is something that you want, above everything else. Those people that choose to be happy will at some point in life wake up to a day filled with smiles, joy, and laughter. If they are lucky, they will remember that day, focus on its high points, and strive to repeat it at some later date. Before too long, another happy day will come to them, seemingly out of the blue. People around them will wonder why they seem to be so different. A new hairdo, dental work, perhaps a new relationship will be pegged as possible reasons for the subtle yet palpable shift.

The reason however, will not be found in surface changes. The newly discovered happiness that now radiates from the aspirants aura was not created by chance. Happiness emerges from the expression of the desire for a happy life.

About the Author

Dr. Mitchell Gibson is the best-selling author of *Your Immortal Body of Light, Signs of Mental Illness, Signs of Psychic and Spiritual Ability, The Living Soul, and Ancient Teaching Stories.* He lives in Summerfield North Carolina with his wife Kathy and two children, Michael and Tiffany.

Contact Information

Tybro Publications
110 Oak Street
High Point NC 27260

Email: mgibsonmd@aol.com
Phone: 336-423-2426

Made in the USA
Monee, IL
09 April 2020